UNDERSTANDING REIKI

Understanding Reiki

Physician Heal Thyself

Raymond R Bullock

CAXTON REFERENCE

© 2001 Caxton Editions

This edition published 2001 by Caxton Publishing Group Ltd,
20 Bloomsbury Street, London, WC1B 3QA.

Design and compilation by The Partnership Publishing Solutions Ltd,
Glasgow, G77 5UN

All rights reserved.
No part of this publication may be reproduced, stored in a retrieval system, or transmitted, in any form or by any means, electronic, mechanical, photocopying, recording or otherwise, without the prior permission of the copyright holder.

Printed and bound in India

DISCLAIMER

This book is meant to be an introduction to Reiki –
it's only purpose is to induce the interested reader to
seek out a qualified Reiki master, and find out more.
It is the author's belief that Reiki can neither be
taught, nor passed on through the written word – this
book does not attempt to do either.

The personal experiences with Reiki have been
honestly presented.

It is important to note that Reiki practitioners do
not claim Reiki to be a substitute for orthodox
medical treatment, but do suggest that it can be used
to complement all treatments, whether they are
conventional or alternative therapies. Therefore, it is
recommended that the reader discuss his or her
condition with their GP, and attain their guidance,
before attempting other methods.

Many of the theories and concepts in this book,
especially for related therapies, are the result of
research and not necessarily the opinions of the
author or publishers.

ABOUT THE AUTHOR

Raymond R Bullock is a poet and writer from the Wirral, currently teaching T'ai Ji Quan and martial arts, as well as Oriental poetry. He also promotes group studies in stress reduction through contemplative writing and T'ai Chi exercises.

After studying at John Moores University in Liverpool he received a degree in Philosophy and Imaginative Writing and a Master's degree in Writing.

His interest in Chinese philosophy and related arts ranges over a thirty-year period, and centres on the study of the I Ching and its use as an instrument in self-development.

Writing interests at the present time include, a study of Traditional Chinese Medicine and its connections with I Ching and T'ai Chi, a collection of Haiku poems and Writing as Therapy.

GRATITUDE LIST

My thanks firstly to Gill Hayes and Pat Power for use of their centre for photographs. The Centre For Holisitic Therapies, the Blackwell Building in Brook Street, Neston on the Wirral (CH649XJ), can be contacted via phone on 0151336 6222 or at **cht@hol-therapy.com** and **www.hol-therapy.com**
    Further thanks to Gill Hayes and Jane Casey (both Reiki exponents) for standing in as models for the pictures, and to Stephen and Vicki Hon for the photo and computer graphics. Thanks to Gill Thurston for attunements, and guidance during the writing of this book and photographic sessions. To Carol Harrison B.Sc. DABCH. MCAHyp. MNGH(USA) for permission to reprint her description of Hynotherapy. (Carol can be contacted via The Centre For Holisitic Therapies, Neston - as above) My thanks to authors and publishers, mentioned in the bibliography and throughout the book, without whom my understanding of Reiki and other therapies would be much narrower.

Thanks also to Professor Yee and the staff and therapists of the Water's Edge Holistic Centre, in New Brighton on the Wirral for various and many occasions of support and guidance. Most especially to Professor Yee for the translation of the T'ai Chi Classic, Chi Gung closing exercise, and for much of my interest in TCM and its connection with the I Ching. Thanks last but not least, to Kam Lau my T'ai Chi instructor, and to Grandmaster Chen Xiaowang, for my continued interest and understanding of Tai Chi.

DEDICATION

I dedicate this book to Jane, Carol, Michelle and Allan for their love and unconditional support; my life is brighter for their presence. Also to Becky, Ashleigh, Adam, Danny, Brandon and all further grandchildren to appear after this book is published, for the same.

Contents

Introduction   17

Chapter 1 Questions on Reiki   21
    What is Reiki?   21
    Where did Reiki come from?   27
    Who can use Reiki?   32
    When can Reiki be used?   33
    How does Reiki affect the giver?   35

Chapter 2 Principles and Chakras   39
    What happens when you have found a guide?   41
    What is a Chakra?   42

Chapter 3 My first Reiki session   47
    First Degree Reiki   49
    A simple daily program   51

Chapter 4 Treatment for others   71

Chapter 5 Other healing sessions   125
Group healing   125
Reiki sessions for animals   129
Reiki sessions for children   131

Chapter 6 Second Degree Healing   133
Reiki for practical use   140

Chapter 7 Other theories and therapies   143
Chi Gung   143
Some useful Chi Gung exercises   145
   Still standing stance   146
   Opening stance   150
   Grounding exercise   158
TCM – Traditional Chinese Medicine   172
T'ai Chi Chuan   177
T'ai Chi Chuan Classic of the Chian-Long Dynasty (1736–1796)   182
Connections between Reiki and the I Ching   187
   About the I Ching   187
   I Ching and Reiki   190

Contents

Spiritual Healing	195
The Christian Healing Ministry	195
Spiritual Healers	198
The National Federation of Spiritualist Healers	198
Ayurvedic mind-body healing	200
Reflexology	203
Shiatsu and Acupressure	204
Homeopathy	205
Hypnotherapy	207
Chapter 8 Case files	**213**
Bibliography	**223**
Suggested Further Reading	**227**

Introduction

Holistic therapies are founded on the principle that sickness results from lack of harmony, between the body, mind and spirit. While a problem can originate in any of these areas, the end product is a lack of power. In the absence of energy the human organism begins to fail.

The body as machine is a complex structure of interrelated processes, each having its own purpose, and functioning as part of the whole.

An extremely sensitive nervous system, controlled by the brain, synchronizes the performance of all of these networks. Some, such as the learning of new tasks, require conscious awareness. Others like the movement of blood through the heart need only an automatic response. Information via the senses is collected and processed at incredible speed, the appropriate reactions being almost immediate. All of this requires energy, which is of course what this book is about.

The many billions of cells that make up the

human organism are dependent on a continuous supply of energy, provided in many ways. The body converts matter to energy, in order that the cells can perform their intricate tasks, but holistic medicine also observes the vital function of the energy known as the life force (Ki in Japanese, Chi in Chinese and Prana in Indian).

Any blockage, excess or deficiency of Ki will result in harm to the cells, and a weakening of the function in the area of damage. If, for instance, this occurs in the internal organs, many other areas of the body are seen to suffer. In holistic medicine this is defined as blockage of the Ki. The flow of this energy throughout the body, just like that of blood as it carries nutrients from food, air and water, must be constant for optimum health.

This does not mean that the physical body is not treated; to the contrary, the holistic therapies described in this book, and many others, employ herbal remedies, massage, physical exercises and breathing techniques. Nevertheless the main action is to restore the balance of Ki.

Some of the above-mentioned methods are dependent on analysis of symptoms; others use exercises to prevent imbalance – Reiki does neither. Reiki works directly with the life force itself, using the oldest and most natural method of healing- touch.

Reiki, as with many of the Eastern healing methods currently in use in the West, comes to us

Introduction

steeped in mystery. There might be as many opinions concerning mysterious knowledge as there are people, but in the main they follow two courses.

For some, imbued with a flair for logic, information that comes wrapped up in ambiguity is at best worthless, at worst outright deception. At the other extreme is the kind of thinking which could be called inspirational: the sort of mind that demands originality and perceives mysterious knowledge as archaic or occult and/or evil in intent. The first leans heavily toward a scientific approach to knowledge, while the second is often religious in its emphasis; there are of course many others in between.

Whether we relate exclusively to either view, we ought to accept that both schools of thought suffer from prejudice. Prejudice can be defined as an incomplete attitude to knowledge, especially knowledge of a different register.

Reiki is this kind of knowledge.

Chapter 1
Questions on Reiki

What is Reiki?

In the main Reiki is a healing art whose name translates as Universal Life Force/ Energy, and involves the act known as – *laying on of hands*. This particular form of healing has its parallel in many religions and societies. The Christian Church, Spiritualist Churches, Taoist, Buddhist and Ayurvedic healers all use, or have used the *hands on* approach to healing.

What separates Reiki from other methods of hands on healing, is the manner in which the ability is passed on.

When the new healer receives energy from the teacher/master, they develop the ability to heal themselves and others. Next they receive the potential to become teachers, and pass on these skills to others.

Many exponents of Reiki claim that the ability to heal in this way is a natural function of all peoples: a function lost as we came to depend on other forms of healing.

For one who heals through Reiki, the function has been restored through a realignment of the life energy. The *Ki* of Rei-ki, is the Japanese name for this energy: in Chinese it is *Chi* and in Indian it is known as *Prana*. This force is essential to a living organism – it is the *life force*: when it departs, death results.

In a functional sense the Rei- of Rei-ki is translated as Universal, but its esoteric meaning is closer to Spiritual Consciousness. Depending on our belief system, we might interpret this as Supernatural Knowledge, Universal Consciousness or God Consciousness.

This meaning alters our viewpoint of the Ki: in this sense it is not that we are conscious of it i.e. through our belief of its existence, it is that *it has its own consciousness*.

When we perform Reiki, all of our personal energies of mind, body and emotion benefit, without need of our conscious direction. The power of Reiki has influence upon our being because of, and through, its own intelligence.

An invisible Aura surrounding the body has been detected via a process called Kirlian photography: this process has revealed striking diagnostic information concerning the presence of diseases such as cancer. Named after the Russian, Semyon Kirlian who discovered it in the 1940s, the procedure demonstrates how patterns of energy surround living things. These patterns of energy are also known as the personal Aura. Electrography, as it is also known, translates electromagnetic fields, surrounding living objects, into a photograph of an electrical corona, or Aura.

While the results of certain studies suggest that Kirlian photography might soon become a valuable diagnostic device, research by Professor Arthur Ellison of City University, London, suggests that the main barrier to this is the vast quantity of variables upon which the result depends.

Two sets of electrographic prints, taken before and after short periods of yoga, demonstrate a deeper more complete aura, after training. A repeat of the test after gymnastic exercise showed no change at all.

It would seem then, that the Aura is a demonstration of the reality of the life force. It is the manifestation of our true state of health or sickness, balance

The Aura demonstrates the reality of the life force: it is the manifestation of our true state of health or sickness, balance or disorder.

The dictionary meaning for Aura is atmosphere, feeling or air- i.e. an *air* of menace; *atmosphere* of sincerity; a *feeling* of discord. Through the Aura we can both reveal our own well-being, as well as sensing the condition of others.

Despite extreme reactions in the West to healing

systems based on such conceptions as described above, there is a section of the medical profession engaged in determined research. These competent and open-minded individuals, view the long established healing methods of the East, with something more than interest.

They find that from the point of view of modern physics, which conceives of matter as energy, far from being archaic these ancient systems hold the key to the medicine of the new millennium. In his foreword to *Vibrational Medicine, New Choices for Healing Ourselves* by Richard Gerber M. D., Professor William A. Tiller Ph. D. states:

> *Now is the time to begin serious investigation of the etheric and to develop an etheric science to balance our present, Physical, material science.*

Gerber depicts the human organism as an interactive series of multidimensional energy fields. This sequence is the aura through which disease can be identified before it has become manifest on a physical level.

Gabriel Cousins M.D. in an introduction to the same book states:

> *We will newly embrace the holistic view that has been with us for thousands of years. It is an understanding that not only does the healer see health from a holistic*

perspective as part of an overall relationship with the universe, but the healer lives as an example of such a whole and harmonious way. I saw this being actively practised by some Ayurvedic physicians in India, and heard about it in Taoist healers, American Indian medicine men/women, and Hunza healers. In our Western culture it has been practised for over two thousand years by the Essenes, who produced such healers as John the Baptist, John the Divine and of course Jesus.

Gerber describes a new medical consensus, which believe that the denial of the existence of the dimension of spirit is a denial of the most essential quality of humankind. His book is an attempt to create a paradigm of a future system of medicine from a synthesis of Eastern and Western medicine.

To sum up: Reiki is a form of healing which utilizes an energy called Ki, in Japanese, which translates as life force. Rei- can mean Universal in a practical sense, and Spiritual Consciousness esoterically. Many other hands on healing systems employ this same energy, to affect a balance and thereby produce protection from disease.

Increasingly, Western Doctors are beginning to treat the human organism in a holistic sense, because of the influence of Eastern methods. This is not to say that Eastern medicine replaces that of the West, only that a synthesis is beginning to form as the result of scientific research.

Questions on Reiki

Where did Reiki come from?

The history of Reiki is in some parts clearly documented, but is always dependent on the opinions and point of view of the historian of whichever text. In the following the reader will find nothing new except, perhaps, for this author's belief in a connection with the history of the I Ching. Here, my concept is that, within the I Ching can be found the fundamental paradigm for what we know as the Reiki healer. I believe that the sage-king, the shaman and the mystical healer of antiquity, who are all found within the I Ching, are equivalents to the Reiki healer.

Dr. Mikao Usui founded Usui Reiki at the end of the nineteenth century. Usui was then the Director and Christian minister at Doshisha University in Kyoto, Japan. While reading to his students on the miracles of Christ' healing, Usui was questioned whether his own belief in Christ's ministry meant that he could imitate these miracles. It is said that Usui was so disturbed by the question that it became his sole mission in life to find the key through which he could replicate these skills.

After applying for direction to the Christian authorities in Japan, he was informed that such healing was neither practised nor spoken of in the Catholic Church.

He then travelled to America where he received a Doctorate in Theology, and among other skills, learned to read Sanskrit, the ancient language of India.

He recognised the similarities in the life of Buddha and Christ, both of whom were able to heal at a touch as well as from great distances.

He decided to widen his search to include ancient Buddhist texts and finally came upon the mantras and symbols, which were the code for what is now Traditional Usui Reiki.

The scriptures, of Tibetan origin, are called the Tantra Lotus Sutra. No instructions or formula, for releasing the force required to heal by touch alone, was incorporated.

Usui spent much time in a Buddhist monastery and after explaining his difficulty to his spiritual Director, was advised to meditate while fasting. This Usui did for twenty-one days on a mountain in Japan called Koriyama. Just before dawn on the final day a great light appeared and struck him in the middle of his forehead. The experience that followed can be described as a spiritual experience.

His inner consciousness was illuminated by what he described as a mass of brightly coloured bubbles. They settled to form the symbols from the Tantra Lotus Sutra. Along with conscious knowledge of how to use this spiritual power, he was endowed with the healing force itself.

In this way Reiki was passed to Mikao Usui, a man whose diligent search resulted in a miracle for him and many others. It is said that Usui 'was touched by God' (or whatever name the reader might prefer) and for this reason further healers required only to be touched, for this healing energy to be passed to them.

At one of his many lectures in Japan, Dr. Usui met a retired Navy Commander, Dr, Chujiro Hayashi. Usui told him he was too young for retirement and enlisted him as his assistant. They toured Japan, demonstrating Reiki healing to others, until Dr. Usui's death in 1930.

Dr. Hayashi opened a clinic in Tokyo were he trained Reiki masters and healed many patients. When he realised that war was imminent, and that his students would probably be conscripted, he decided to pass on his teachings to his wife Chie Hayashi and one of his former patients, Hawayo Takata.

Hawayo Takata was born in Hawaii of poor parents and spent most of her early years working on a plantation. She married an accountant in 1917 and had two children, both girls. After the untimely death of her husband from a heart attack, she had to work long hours to feed and house her family. The result of the excess work brought on severe ill health and she was diagnosed with a tumour, nervous exhaustion and gallstones.

The hospital felt that, in her critical condition, it would be dangerous to operate. They strongly suggested that she rest and recuperate her strength, under hospital supervision, and she did so for some weeks.

On the eve of her scheduled operation an inner voice told her that the operation was unnecessary. She tried to ignore it, but the voice persisted and she asked the surgeon if there was any other method of cure. The surgeon told her of Hayashi's clinic, where his sister been both healed and trained, and recommended that Mrs. Takata listen to her inner voice, and go there.

She remained at the clinic, receiving treatment for four months, and eventually was well enough to leave. Mrs. Takata asked to stay on and be initiated into Reiki, but was at first refused because she was not Japanese. She persisted however and Dr. Hayashi relented. She received her Reiki One attunement in 1936 and Reiki Two the following year.

Mrs. Takata and Dr. Hayashi began to lecture in Hawaii, demonstrating the effectiveness of Reiki. She opened her own clinic in 1938 with the aid of Dr. Hayashi, after she had received her Reiki Three attunement.

Dr Hayashi had already been drafted but since he had become a healer, taking life was impossible for him. It is claimed that he stopped his own heart on May 10, 1941 choosing to die rather than violate the principles of Reiki.

In 1941 Mrs. Takata became the successor to Chujiro Hayashi. She travelled to Canada and America, initiating many new healers and personally healing the sick. She taught in a manner she thought best suited to each student, altering the hand positions and symbols, as she believed necessary.

Mrs. Takata died in 1980, on December 11th. Because of her devotion to Reiki and its principles and the passion of her ministry, there are estimated to be around five thousand or more Reiki masters and half a million practitioners worldwide.

Who can use Reiki?

It appears that anyone, with enough willingness to accept responsibility for his/her own health, can become a Reiki healer. The transference of the ability to heal is not dependent on intellectual or spiritual capacity. It is not required that one follows any particular faith and background or culture have no significance whatsoever. All that appears to be required is a desire to heal and be well.

In order to promote spiritual balance in the Reiki art, Usui developed a number of Reiki principles (see below). These should not be thought of as rules, they are spiritual principles or ideals that the practitioner is expected to work towards.

When can Reiki be used?

As a healing process Reiki is generally used as a complementary treatment to other methods. Reiki practitioners believe that not all medical problems are physical only; some are based in emotional and mental disorders whose source might be difficult to discover. A period of sharing between patient and healer might be necessary in order to create a relaxed atmosphere.

It should also be understood that many diseases are a result of spiritual blockages, and that the mental, physical and emotional symptoms will continue until the root cause of the dis-ease is confronted.

While Reiki does not depend on analysis for its effects on the recipient, if the difficulties are recurrent, it benefits everyone to have some understanding of the human condition.

As the primary purpose of Reiki is to allow the healer to become a channel for the energy known as Ki, we need to recognize some of the effects this might have on the practitioner and patient alike.

Some of the obvious effects can be irritability and discomfort expressed in many ways. For instance, those difficulties resulting from suppression of emotional trauma can manifest in the form of sobbing or anger when released. These are only symptoms of the disorder, and as such we ought to recognise that they are in fact, expressions of the healing process.

Other symptoms may manifest in a mental form, as resentful or self-pitying thought patterns. Again, these are expressed as a result of the healing process. We ought to be aware, as practitioners, that this is a holistic healing process and that if we do not feel capable of counselling the patient in a positive way, we ought to pass him or her on to someone who does.

The primary concern here is that, whoever the receiver might be, we ought to be ready, and more importantly capable of, participation in the process of recovery.

Many healings are simple and require only a single session to induce recovery. These would be in the nature of purely physical problems, such as calming those suffering from shock or aiding in the cessation of blood flow from open wounds. Relief from pain is also a common result from a Reiki session.

Self-healing works in the same way: I find that Reiki can relieve a tormenting headache almost immediately.

How does Reiki affect the giver?

As Reiki practitioners are channels only, their personal energy is unaffected by a session of healing. Unlike many of our altruistic activities, Reiki is not performed as an act of will, rather as an act of submission. We open up to the force and guidance of whatever we consider to be the source of the Universal Energy, Ki, Chi or Prana etc. and allow this intelligence to activate the healing.

The very act of submission might be our first act of self-sacrifice, and therefore the beginning of a journey of personal discovery and expansion.

Nevertheless, healing is but a small part of the development we can expect once we become attuned to the spiritual path.

The terms self and personality define the human attributes necessary for survival of the individual, and while this can also include others, it generally does so as a closed belief system (see the chapter on the I Ching).

A closed system is basically one in which we move from one extreme to its opposite, or what we perceive as its opposite, to effect a solution. For example, perceiving a weakness within ourselves, we might develop aggressive tendencies as a counter irritant, or vice versa, always returning to the opposite after each subsequent failure. We then inject more energy into our new venture, until the whole structure collapses around us.

When these closed systems have been pre-created through dogma, habit or prejudicial beliefs, there is little likelihood we can avoid the eventual disintegration. This is so because we have no exit through which to escape.

At the other extreme we have our metaphysical requirements, most often expressed through our religions. These too are necessary for the survival and growth of the species, but again suffer from the closed structure syndrome.

The problems created by closed structures have been defined, elsewhere, as the sum total of human disease.

Reiki, and other related processes, are the doors to our release from these maladies. They provide the new and different perspectives that point the way to an escape, from self-centredness and fear, to development of the higher attributes. I should stress that these processes can only remove the blocks to growth. Self-development is a consequence of continuously trying to function in this new perspective.

What we must also remember is that these processes can also degenerate into closed structures. As human beings we are dependent on solutions. When we find one that works we like to imagine we have resolved all of our dilemmas.

This probably signifies why they flourish for a

while throughout history, and are then lost, to return only through diligent search and insight.

CHAPTER 2
Principles and Chakras

The Traditional Reiki Principles are defined as:

Just for today I will be grateful for my many blessings
Just for today I will not worry
Just for today I will not be angry
Just for today I will labour honestly
And will act with kindness to my neighbour

The primary benefit of living by such principles is that, as we attune to the flow of energy, we find we no longer project, negatively, into tomorrow: today's gifts are more than sufficient for our requirements.

Just for today we recognise our limitations as they apply in our living experience, and allow the intelligent force we call, in this instance, Reiki, to expand our acceptance of life. After all what is worry and anger if not an inability to accept what is?

The Reiki principles then are ideals that we can work towards, keeping in mind that it is the willingness to do so, despite personal limitations, that makes self-development possible.

A book, any book (including this one) cannot teach you Reiki. In fact, it could increase your confusion. To begin then, we must seek out a Reiki Master.

This is simpler than it might seem, Reiki healers do not hide away. In fact you can probably find one or two in Yellow Pages, and many more through the Internet.

Despite the fact that Reiki, as a healing art, has been in the West for a very short time, there are many thousands of genuine teachers. They can be found throughout most of Europe, America and Australia. There are many established groups of Reiki Masters and students, who practise both the traditional Reiki system as well as innovative teachings. No matter what the content of the school, each is obedient to the same power for healing.

You will find that there are also many Reiki Master/Teachers who are not affiliated to any school, but they are still a part of the tradition of Reiki.

What happens now that you have found a guide?

This is where the student is introduced to Reiki One. This is the beginners level at which the student experiences the first opening of the channels. We should know therefore what this opening, or attunement comprises, and also something of the nature of the channels themselves, and to do this we must speak of Chakras.

What is a Chakra?

The Tantra Lotus Sutra was the Tibetan Buddhist formula for what is now known as Reiki. They put down a set of Symbols to be included with sound, in the form of Mantras, through which the energy channels might be opened. This enhanced energy flow enabled the body's natural healing abilities to activate.

The Mantra is a rhythmic repetition of a name, and the symbol is its written representative.

The channels begin to vibrate as a result of this concentration, and the Chakras increase in energy. Chakras are energy centres and there are seven of these. As a Reiki healing session begins at the head we can imagine gently placing the hands over these points.

The throat Chakra is at the lowest point of the neck and its colour is pale blue. In this hollow the energy centre for the thyroid and parathyroid gland, the throat and upper lungs, nestles between the collar bones and functions as a communication centre in every sense. Higher and Lower selves are expressed through this centre, as is our individuality, creativity and emotional drives.

The highest energy point is the Crown Chakra. Placed approximately where the hair spirals from just behind the topmost point of the head, and it is through here that one receives the Chi or Ki.

Principles and Chakras

Connected to the pineal gland and upper brain, its colour is white and is associated with spirituality, wisdom and intuition.

Next at the point between the eyes is the Third Eye or Brow Chakra, whose physical connections are to the lower brain and pituitary gland. Its colour is indigo and is associated with clairvoyance and willpower. Therefore, our inner realities good or bad are created here. It is also the Chakra through which we achieve spiritual awakening as we open up to the Greater Will.

The throat Chakra is at the lowest point of the neck and its colour is pale blue. In this hollow the energy centre for the thyroid and parathyroid gland, the throat and upper lungs, nestles between the collar bones and functions as a communication centre in every sense. Higher and Lower selves are expressed through this centre, as is our individuality, creativity and emotional drives.

The heart Chakra houses the energy for the heart, thymus gland and lower lungs and its colour is green. The energy for the circulation of blood, for the emotions, for love, compassion and spiritual development, is in this energy centre.

The next energy centre is found in the solar plexus, where the energy for liver, stomach, gall bladder, pancreas and solar plexus is situated. From here comes the sense of power and strength. Fear is also seated here. Its colour is the yellow of the sun and its influence spreads out in a similar way.

The sacral Chakra is orange and is the centre for the spleen, urogenital system, kidneys and male and female reproductive organs. It is the centre for vital energy, self-worth and desire and is placed just below the navel.

Principles and Chakras

Finally we have the root Chakra found at the lowest point of the body, at the genital area, and is bright red in colour. Here is the energy for the bladder, adrenals genitals and spine, where all the most basic of instincts, like survival and procreation receive their energy.

The above Chakras are the seven primary energy centres. There are many other Chakras, but these are called minor Chakras.

CHAPTER 3
My first Reiki healing session

My introduction to Reiki was at the Holisitic Centre, in Neston with Reiki master, Jill Thurston. The meeting had been arranged by phone so we had not met up to that point. It was an energetic phone call lasting almost two hours.

I had heard of some of the effects of a session from friends involved with Reiki, and of course had read much through research of alternative therapies. As I understood it the effects would be of the purgative nature, and primarily physical. I had been involved with Yoga and Chi Gung for some years at this stage, and felt that I was unlikely to have much left to purge.

When the time for the session arrived, a vibrant lady, exhibiting vast amounts of vital energy, confronted me. The Neston Centre is one of those extremely relaxed, welcoming places; havens for those looking for a little sanctuary. My new friend moved around it like a whirlwind; not what I had expected.

We spent some time in discussion and general conversation, which I took to be part of the process, then moved on to the hands on session. Jill began with some Aura Soma oils, and I lay down and relaxed.

After the third head position, I felt the heat from her hands on my forehead, then a jolt in my arms, and I fell asleep. Perhaps sleep is the wrong word. The feeling was more elusive, like the state between waking and sleep. A daze, in which I occasionally caught myself snoring. At these times the feeling was that I was fully awake, that I was in the room, but then I would snore again.

When the session was over, the sensation was more like the feeling after the Yoga exercise called, savasana: like standing a little off the floor, or to the side of myself: a sense of being displaced.

I also found logical conversation somewhat difficult, so I thought it wise to relax for a while before attempting to drive home.

There were further effects, this time of the physical kind, when I arrived home. I was overwhelmed by an extreme case of diarrhoea, demonstrating the immediate purgative effects of Reiki. Headaches and archetypal dreams followed.

First Degree Reiki

When we begin to use Reiki One as a hands-on healing process, we ought to keep in mind the necessity to relax.

In T'ai Chi we speak of intention. As we move we direct the flow of Chi to a particular part of the body, whether to the TanTien (Sacral Chakra), or the hands or feet. The intention of the movement might be to push, punch or grab, but we do not finish the move: therefore there is no tension, only intention. It is this intention or meaning, which is also used in Reiki.

When we receive an attunement from our chosen guide, what we are accepting is a transmission of Ki or universal Energy from them. They are the channels, we the recipients. This awakens our innate ability to heal by altering the vibrations of the Chakras. As the vibrations are altered, more Ki flows through the recipient.

It is the vibrations of the Crown, third eye, throat and heart Charkas that are raised, and this enables the new healer to use Reiki primarily for physical ailments.

A further part of this initial training is the use of the hand positions.

Various reactions to this initial laying on of hands are reported. As has already been stated, problems that have been suppressed often surface, and in a variety of ways. If we view each difficulty as an accumulation of toxic waste, then it is not difficult to see in what ways we might be affected.

Physically we might sweat, experience diarrhoea, or possibly even need to vomit in extreme circumstances. Emotional reactions might be just as violent, or so slight as to be unnoticeable. A variety of mental reactions such as resentful, self-pitying thought patterns might surface to overwhelm us. The reactions could be all, but might equally be none of these. All we need remember is that this is a cleansing process, and as such is a beneficial experience.

Chi gung (which we will speak of later) is a similar skill to Reiki and is a fundamental part of T'ai Chi. Hand movements are used, in the first instance, to direct the force of Chi and are practised until the flow of energy becomes automatic. We then need only to intend the Chi to flow for this to take place. It is the same with Reiki healing: we mean/intend it to flow and the intelligent energy does the rest.

Practice is required, therefore, for the flow to become automatic and I suggest the following simple program.

A simple daily program

Each morning you can use your awakening Reiki skills to start your day with positive affirmations. Begin by verbalising your Reiki Principles:

> *Just for THIS day I will accept happiness*
> *And for THIS day accept gratitude*
> *And forego all those negative impulses like anger and worry*
> *I will live in THIS day reaching out to others with love and tolerance*
> *Just for today...*

That last line ought to cover any other devotions required by individual beliefs or religion. Reiki is not the result of one belief, nor is its effectiveness increased or diminished by any religion: the energy it employs is universal and can only be blocked by an attitude of contempt prior to investigation.

After utilize these devotions and attaining a positive attitude, begin to apply the hand positions, to yourself, in the manner taught.

I must stress that to begin with; the hand positions should be in the way they were passed on to you by your teacher. Remember though, that intuition is an important part of Reiki healing, and a little at a time, you will become accustomed to following it. Eventually you will come to depend on it.

Remember also that healing begins with the front

of the head and moves down to the feet, then continues in the same way at the back.

Both hands are turned palm down with the fingers and thumb of each hand touching. No pressure is applied; you need touch each area only gently to receive the desired effect.

In the opening position the hands are placed over the eyes and are slightly cupped. As the energy flows into the hands, it may be experienced as heat or even a tingling sensation. Leave the hands in this way until the sensations diminish. You will note that this position covers the Brow Chakra and is useful for increasing the flow of energy to this point. It can be used for a variety of simple problems such as headache, eyestrain and stress.

My first Reiki healing session

When moving to the next position lower the hands slowly until they are positioned at each cheek with the fingertips touching the temples. Hold your hands this way, until you experience a deep calmness.

A sense of comfort will permeate through the whole body if you are patient with this exercise, and all manner of simple ailments are healed by it such as earache, and cold and flu symptoms.

One need never again depend on powders and pills for pain relief.

My first Reiki healing session

Next relax the shoulders and slide the hands gently to the back of the head. The palms are placed, comfortably above and below the occipital ridge, as if supporting the weight of the whole head.

The Crown and Brow Chakras benefit directly from this position and difficulties such as insomnia, headache, worry and stress are greatly relieved.

My first Reiki healing session

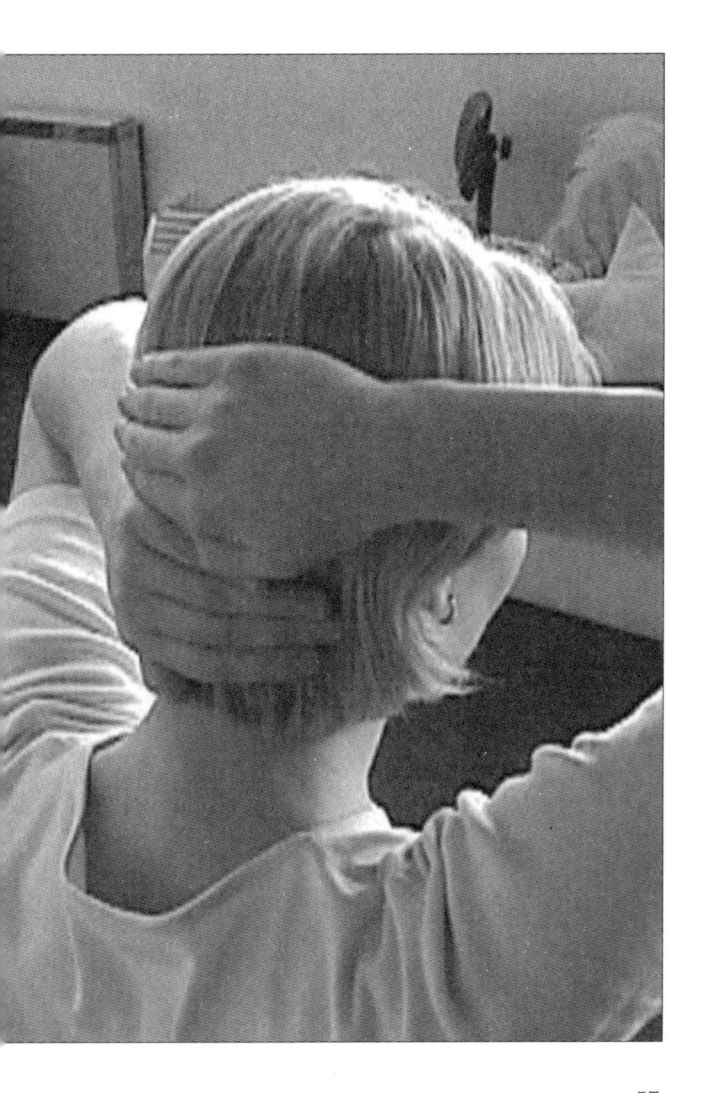

Now move one hand to the brow Chakra and hold the position for a few minutes.

After some practise you will notice that both hands heat up fairly quickly.

My first Reiki healing session

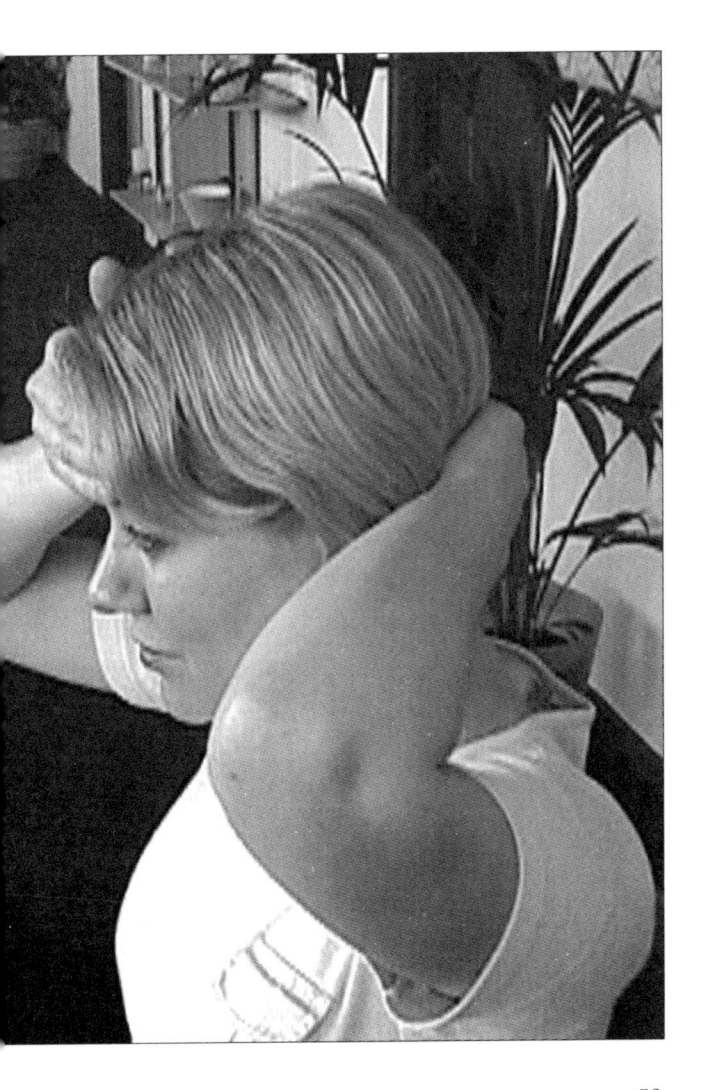

Allow the hands to fall to the base of the skull then draw them gently to the front of the neck and the throat Chakra. Hold this position until the energies vanish before sinking the hands to the next position.

The most obvious results from this position are in the throat itself. Soreness and irritability are relieved. Whether the difficulty is due to cold or flu symptoms, or because of atmospheric problems, the effects are reduced noticeably. Neck pains can also be eased, but if these are persistent, one ought to seek the help of a chiropractor or physician.

My first Reiki healing session

From the throat Chakra lower the elbows until the hands are placed each side of the chest, above the heart.

Here the immediate benefits are a feeling of happiness and joy rising from the heart, and a falling away of negativity. Blood pressure is regulated and the immune system strengthened.

If one imagines love rising from the lowest point of the heart and enveloping the hands, an overwhelming sense of well being often results.

My first Reiki healing session

The hands now drop to waist level so that the tips of the fingers almost touch over the navel. The pancreas is treated with energy from this position and helps to regulate digestion and fat metabolism.

If you are very flexible you could now move to the back. This is a difficult area to work on for obvious reasons, but after some practise the positions become more comfortable.

Place the hands on the large muscles at the shoulders. It is here where the major effects of physical stress are held. Sitting at a desk or computer for long periods of time creates great tension here. If this is your situation, take regular breaks and practise this exercise and the previous one for amazing relief. If you work in an office, after the first session, all of your colleagues will become devotees of Reiki.

My first Reiki healing session

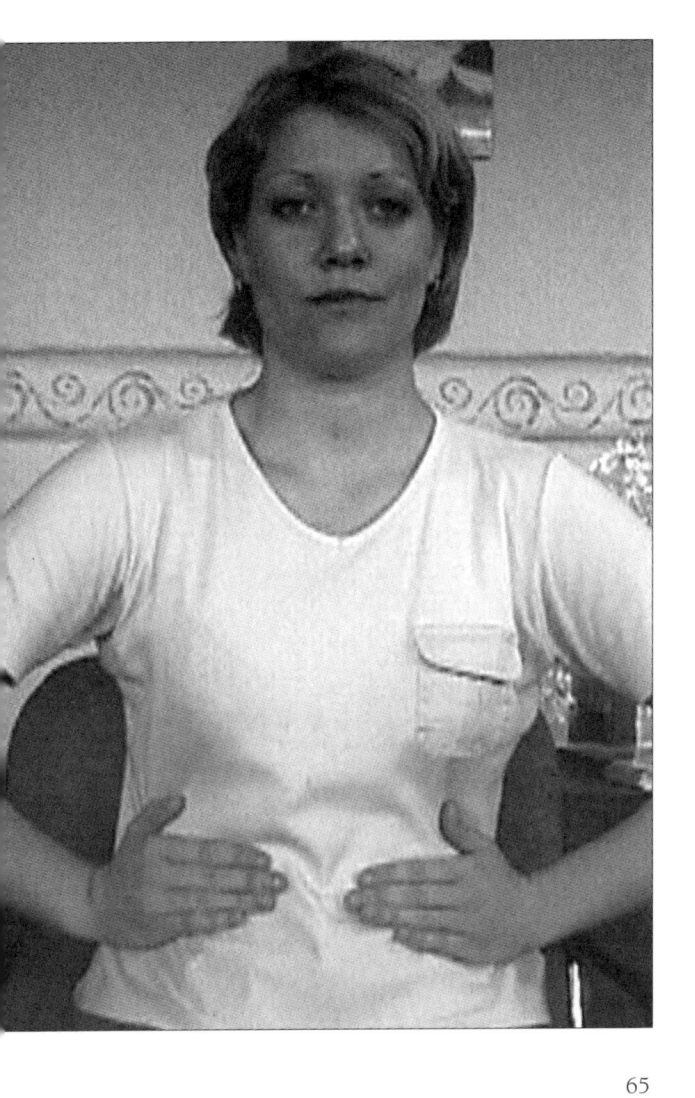

Lower the hands gently to cover the adrenal and kidney area and the sacral Chakra.

Any lower back or problem in the lumbar region of the spine will become evident after working this area. If the condition does not ease, or worsens, again I suggest a visit to your physician.

My first Reiki healing session

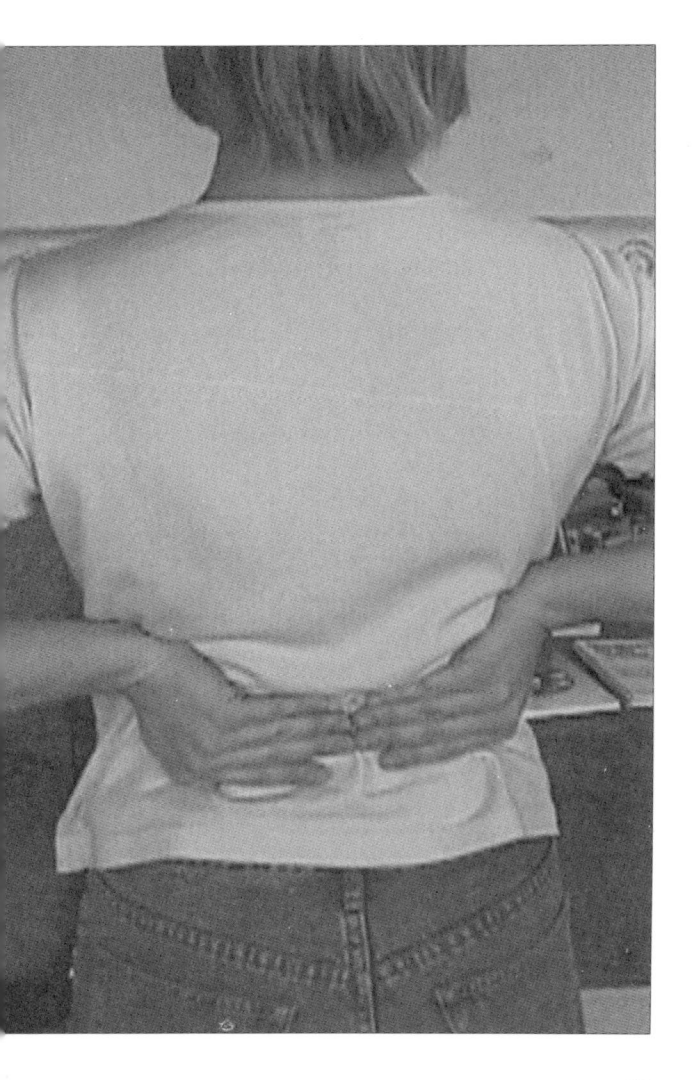

Following the self-healing session, if time allows, rest for a while in a seated position. Keep a pen and paper next to you and take note of the more obvious changes. Should any of the apparently negative symptoms arise, simply take note of them and return to your resting position. Don't try to suppress these reactions, give them fair note and move on. The more information you get from these sessions about yourself, the more useful you will become to your patients.

Repeat your Reiki Principles, especially regarding your Gratitude for your many blessings. This will provide you with a positive frame of mind for the day.

Finally if there is anything of importance, whether disturbing or otherwise, try to find someone in whom you can trust and discuss your findings. This might be your Reiki teacher, a close friend or your physician. Do not be afraid to approach professional people if you feel they can be of use.

Receiving Level One from Reiki Master Jill Thurston was an enlightening experience. We spent some time discussing the principles involved, and the use of relaxing aids such as Aurasoma, and then she suggested I remove my shoes and any jewellery such as rings and watches.

I was seated on a straight-backed chair, eyes closed, while Jill went through the ceremony.

Through this ceremony I would become a channel for the healing energy, able to apply this energy to

My first Reiki healing session

others or myself. Jill performed the attunement in the predetermined manner, using the symbols and hand motions to realign my energies. This rearrangement of my energy patterns would be a permanent feature to be used at any time.

It is worth noting here that the force known as Reiki is of a benevolent nature, and cannot be used to create anything other than well-being. The symbols mentioned above have, until recently, been a well-kept secret. This is not because of a fear that Reiki energy might be used for the wrong purposes: its nature prevents this. The concern has been to prevent those who have not been through the attunement process, using the symbols and professing that they have.

Chapter 4
Treatment for others

As I suggested at the end of the last chapter, attaining as much information from your sessions as possible will improve your understanding of the difficulties of your patients.

While it is necessary to approach your patients with sympathy and understanding, it is more important to treat their confidences with as much objectivity as possible. This is likely to come more naturally if you have become accustomed to sharing your own problematic reactions.

This is an indispensable part of the journey of self-development that you began, when you allowed your Reiki teacher to alter your energy balance.

On this journey you will perceive many blocks to physical, mental and spiritual health that you will naturally want to remove. After all who can continue on such a journey weighed down by burning resentments or self-pity. Some are plagued by these or other, equally powerful reactions to life. Does this mean that they are unable to become healers? Some say it does, that the barriers are too great. I believe that such difficulties pose no problem at all, that this is exactly the kind of problem that Reiki works best at.

In our healing sessions we need to note the nature of the problem, confront it directly and with as much objectivity as possible, in order to allow a full healing of the condition. It benefits nobody, particularly the recipient, if they return to you continuously with the same difficulty. Such dependencies are unhealthy and based on fear. Reiki's purpose is to provide freedom from disease, in all of its manifestations.

We experience something of true freedom, when we recognise that we are totally responsible for our own well being. Conversely, we are also responsible for showing others that this freedom exists, and that it is possible for anyone. We are not responsible for their well being however, and I think that this philosophy is at the heart of Reiki.

It is with this attitude that we approach our patient, remembering again the principle of Gratitude. It is only then that we can further expand our understanding, as we share their difficulties, with a positive frame of mind.

So now to deal with our first Reiki healing session: mostly, preparation is not essential – but it is desirable. I say this because the session may be

Treatment for others

something of an emergency. Your patient may have an open wound or some other problem, which requires immediate assistance. Attend to the emergency in whatever way is required, bandage the wound or call the emergency services if necessary. If the patient is suffering from shock, Reiki can be of use until they arrive. This is only to demonstrate that for Reiki to work, preparations are not needed.

If this is not the case and your patient has booked a session with you, then there are some arrangements that it is only good manners to make.

Think about the senses first. Do you or your clothes smell of tobacco or food; do you wear strong scent; does your chosen room smell of strong herbs, which you enjoy but your patient might find distracting?

Think of the colours of the room, the light and the general look of the room. Is it physically comfortable? Do you intend to work in silence or use soothing music? Are you and you patient agreed on what is soothing?

Some styles of music work on different Chakras – it is useful, for yourself and others, to find out more of this.

Showering before a session might make you feel brighter and more attentive, and having fresh air in the room could also be useful.

I will repeat – that these preparations are not essential, and too much emphasis on them can only result in discomfort, for you and your patient.

Remembering that the purpose of the session is to allow healing energy to pass through you, to use you as a channel – and you will provide yourself with the correct attitude.

While certain kinds of preparation are not necessary to induce healing, there are some that are advisable for other reasons.

Consider the powerful nature of many of the ailments and also the power of the forces for which you have chosen to be a channel. It makes sense in the light of such powerful energies to cleanse yourself in like ways.

If you are used to prayer or meditation, use these fine exercises to prepare yourself; if not simply relax and silently repeat some, or all, of the Reiki Principles. Use the grounding exercise, or one of the simple Chi Gung exercises to centre and relax yourself. These exercises also help to open the channels and provide a confident attitude to the session.

Remove all jewellery and provide a warm environment. Though it was necessary in self-healing to cross one leg over the other to reach the feet, this is not so when healing another. (In T'ai Chi we throw the joints open, to allow for the free movement of Chi.)

Now prepare your patient. Inform them, in a positive and supportive way of the possibility of the

Treatment for others

reactions we have discussed. Explain this in such a way that he or she will not be disturbed by the possibility; will in fact view it as an important part of the healing session. You are now ready to begin.

Have your patient lie down on a treatment table and begin with the manipulation of the aura. This is a simple exercise; hold both of you're a few inches above the Crown Chakra and then move along the body to the feet. At all times keep the hands the same distance from the body. This is a gentling action to enable a bond to pass between yourself and the recipient, and to allow them a sense of security.

First position

With the recipient lying face up on the treatment table, you stand directly behind. Now place your hands above the eyes, then, slowly lower them until gentle contact is made. The fingers are each side of the nose, the palms cupped over the eyes, and the thumbs almost touch at the Third Eye point. Keep the hands in this position until the energy subsides before moving on. The pituitary and pineal glands are flushed with energy and both sides of the brain are balanced.

Use this for treating disorders such as cold symptoms, sinus and/or eye problems, stress and allergies. If the patient experiences any reactions to the first contact, speak calmly and remind him or her that these are signs of recovery. If you have already gained their trust, they will relax again.

Treatment for others

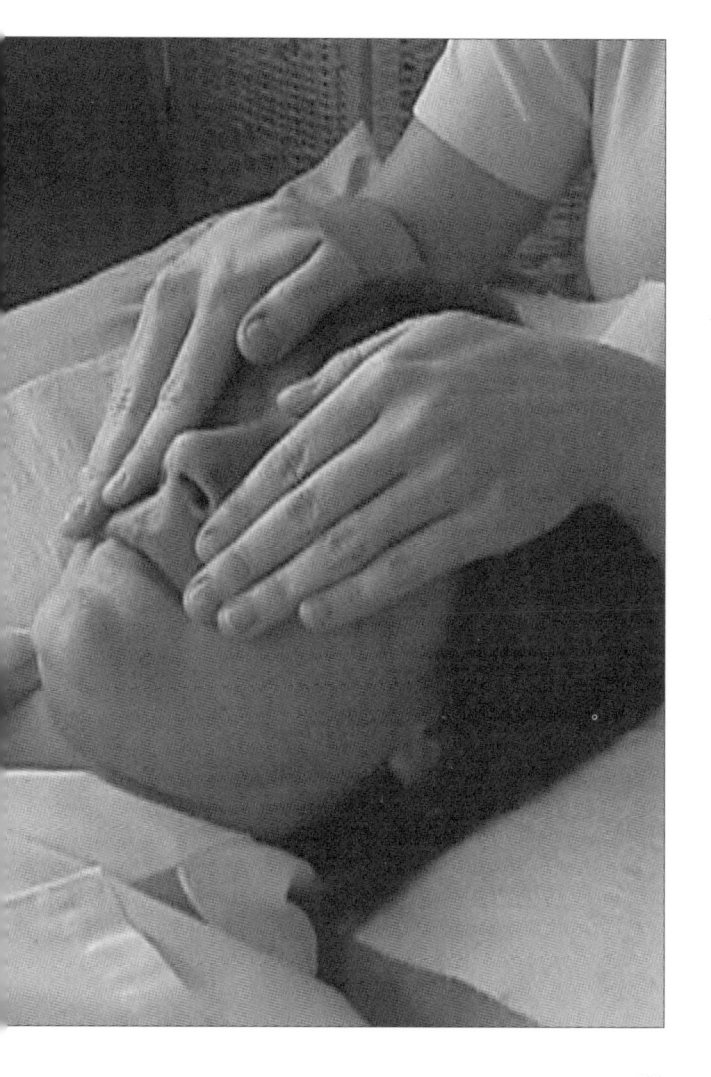

Second position

Keeping gentle contact with the recipient, slide the hands downwards until the cupped palms cover the ears, fingers along the cheeks and base of the thumb touching the temples. The Crown and Brow Chakras both receive attention from this exercise, and if the patient experienced difficulties with the first position, they will usually receive relief at this point. They may become so relaxed that they fall asleep.

As well as calming the mind it is also good for stress and improving memory, concentration and meditation. Cold and flu symptoms and ear, nose and throat difficulties are usually eased by this position. You may also find that older people have improved balance after regular treatments.

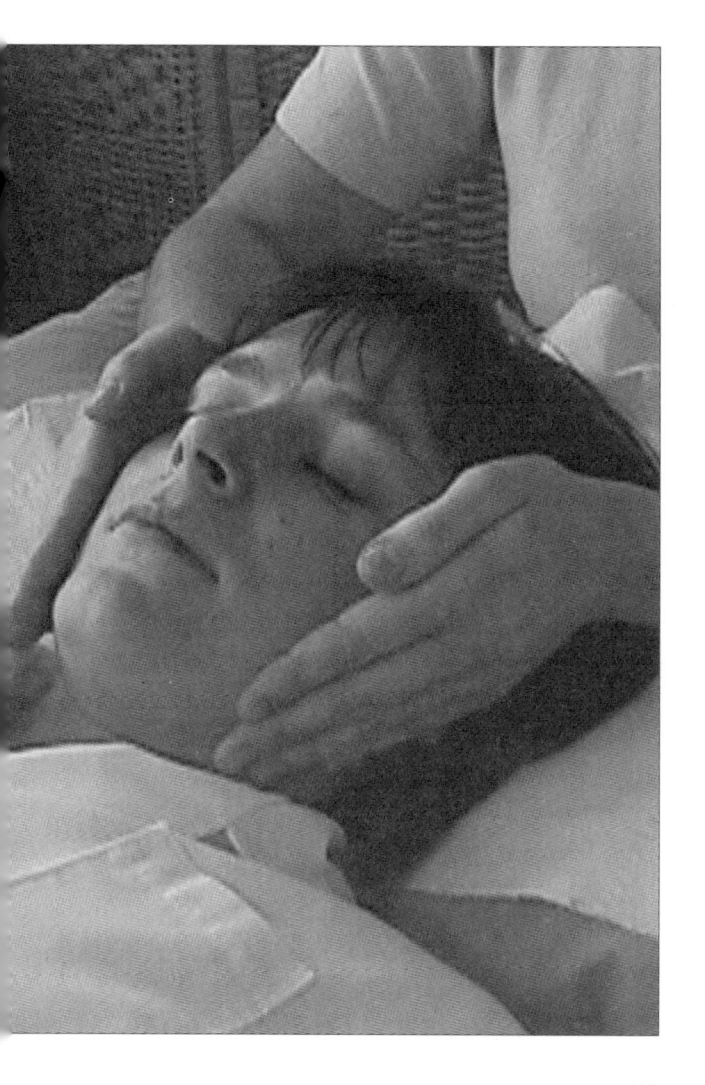

Treatment for others

Third position

Allow the fingers of both hands to slip under the neck until you find the occipital ridge. With some help from the patient, lift the head and slide the palms underneath, then rest the hands on the table. Again the Crown and Brow Chakras receive attention.

Physically the central nervous system and back of the head benefit the most. The position is excellent for reducing fearful reactions, tension headaches and allergies.

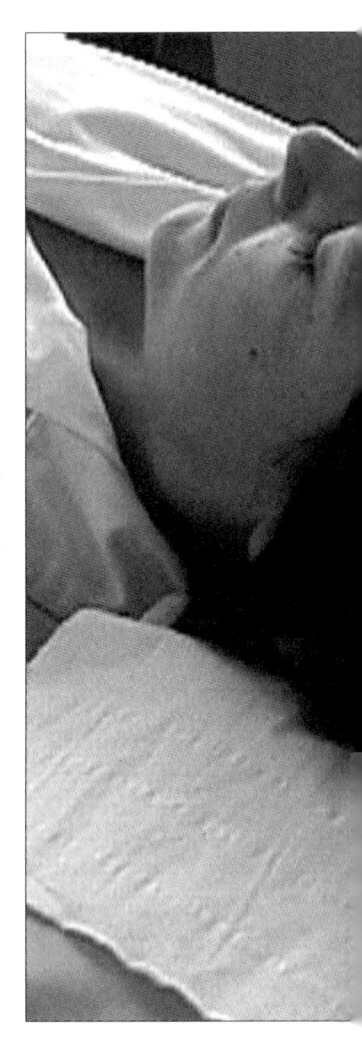

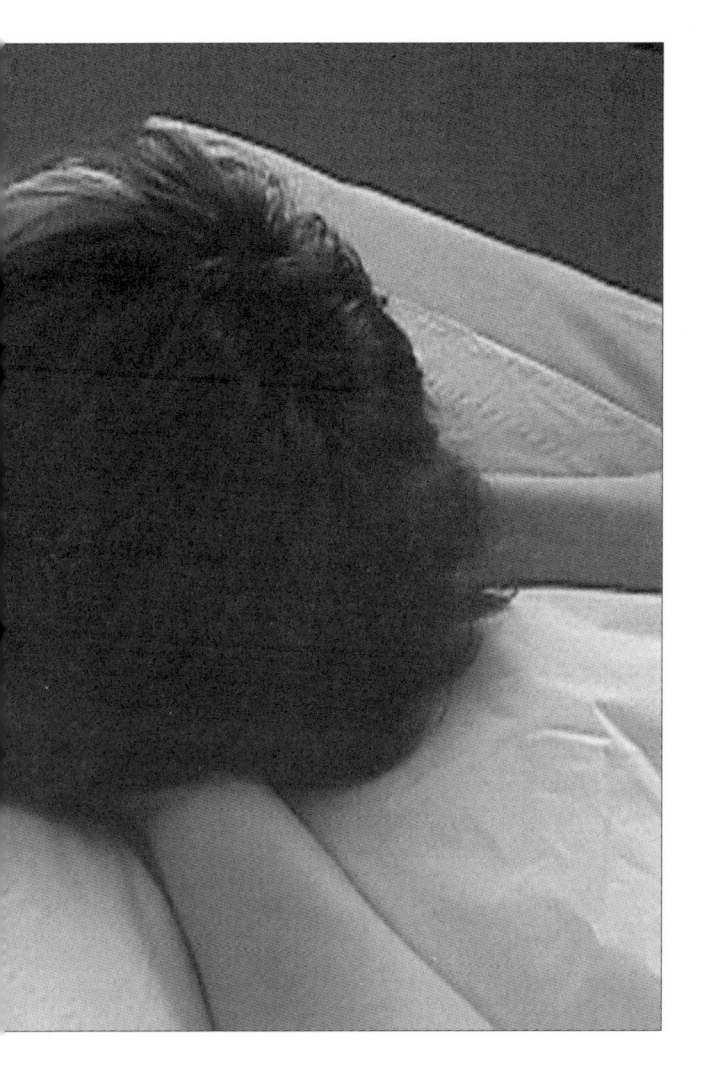

Treatment for others

Fourth position

Relax the wrists, so that you can slip the fingers from beneath the head of the patient, then slide the fingers across the cheeks and down toward the throat. Unless you know you patient well, it is best not to place the hands directly across the throat. Many people have a nervous reaction to this, and you may have to turn the heels of the palms outward to touch the sides of the neck. With the fingers touching the collarbone, the Throat Chakra will receive benefit anyway.

The parathyroid and thyroid glands, lymph nodes and vocal area receive the greatest physical benefit. Throat problems such as tonsillitis, soreness resulting from colds and flu, as well as atmospheric causes all profit this position. Remember that many emotional problems; traumas and suppressed anger, as well as grief, are held here and this is another area where you may observe immediate reactions. It will improve the bond between yourself and the patient if you are both objective and understanding. Suggest that you can both spend time in discussion when the full session is over.

Treatment for others

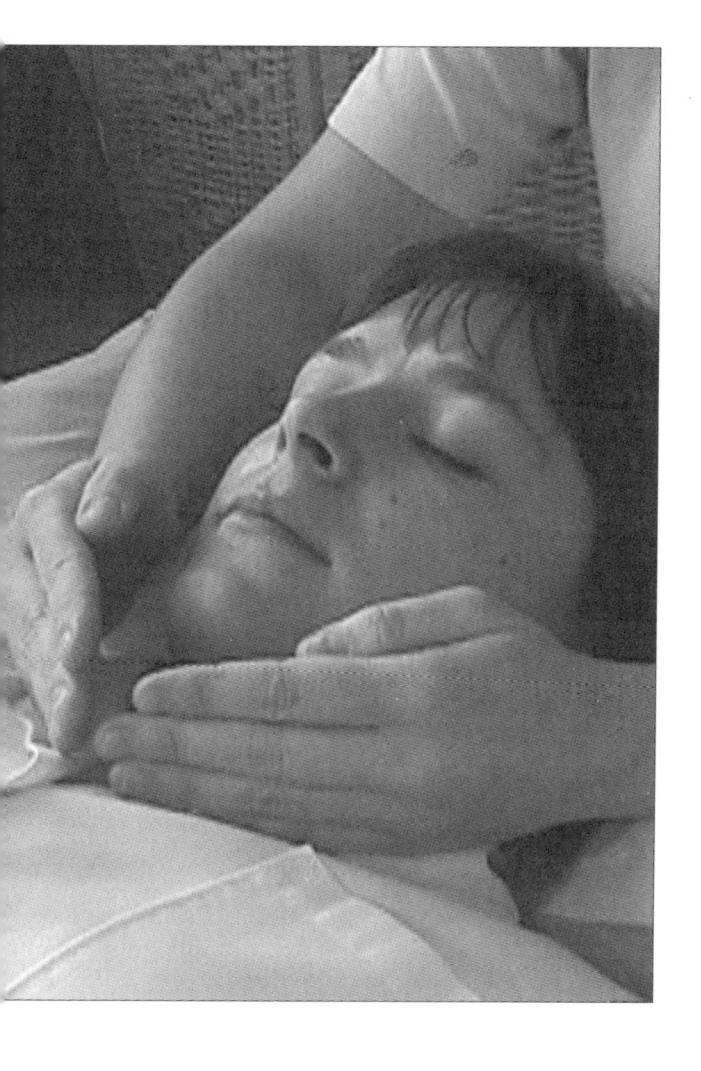

Now we treat the front of the body.

Move around from the last position, turning the hands so that they lie under the collarbone.

This is the Heart Chakra and the heart, lungs and thymus receive greatest benefit. When tension rises in the chest, breathing becomes shallower, creating more tension. This exercise relieves pressure on the lungs and so on all of the chest area, not the least the heart. The immune and lymphatic systems also receive energy from this position.

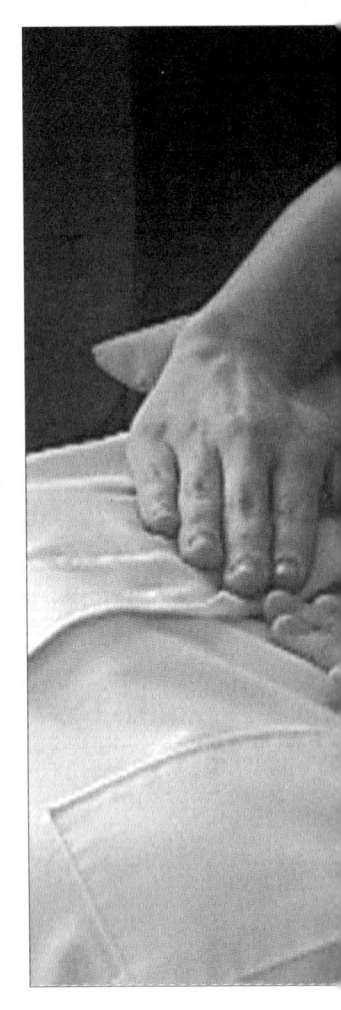

Treatment for others

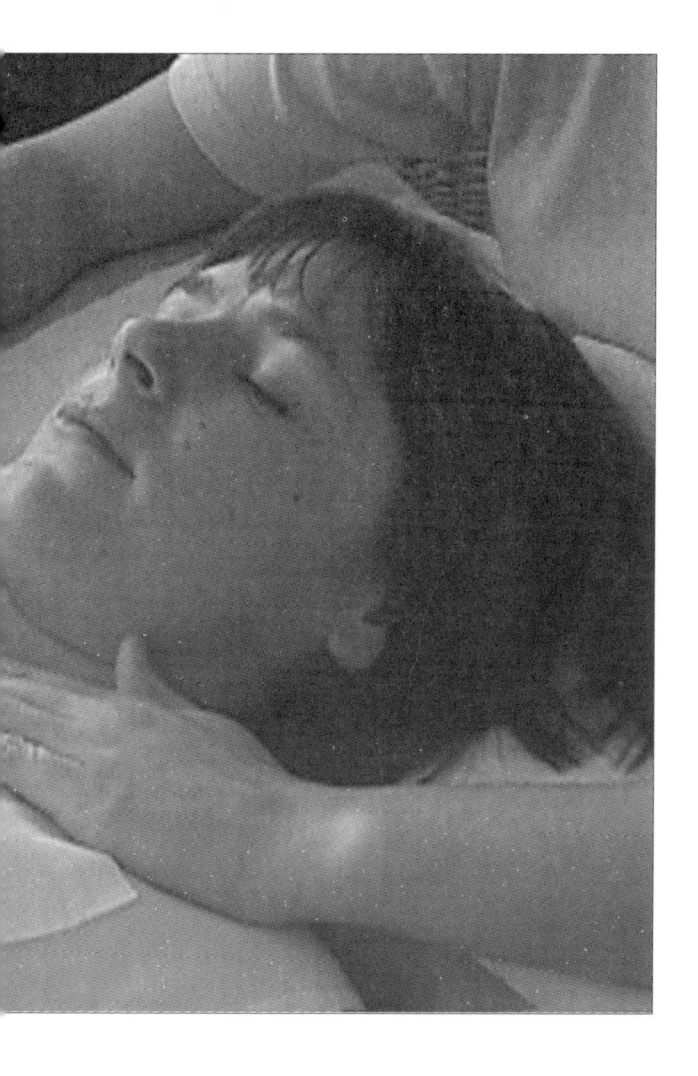

Second position Front

Lower the hands to just below the ribs, on one side of the body, both hands next to each other. Repeat on both sides of the body. The Solar Plexus Chakra is covered.

On the right side the liver, gallbladder and pancreas are treated. Some of the stomach and large intestine are dealt with as well as the duodenum. Physical problems in the digestive tract receive a great deal of benefit, as do difficulties in all of the major organs. Emotional problems, which result from an imbalance in these areas, tend to be relieved after only a few sessions. On the left side the spleen, pancreas and the rest of the stomach and large intestine are affected. The immune system receives a balance in extreme disorders like cancer. For both sides infection of the digestive area are treated.

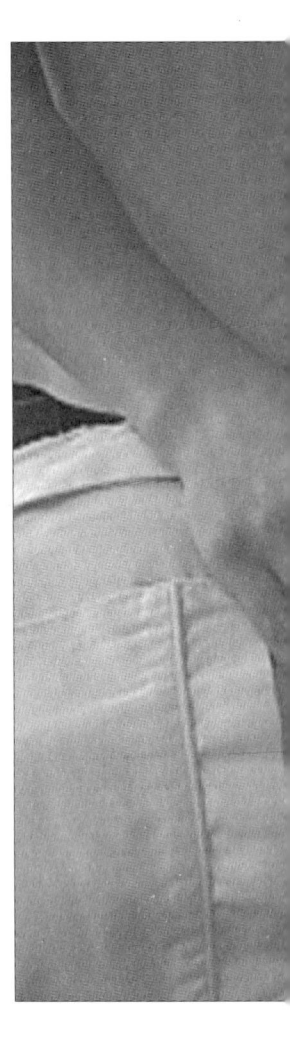

Treatment for others

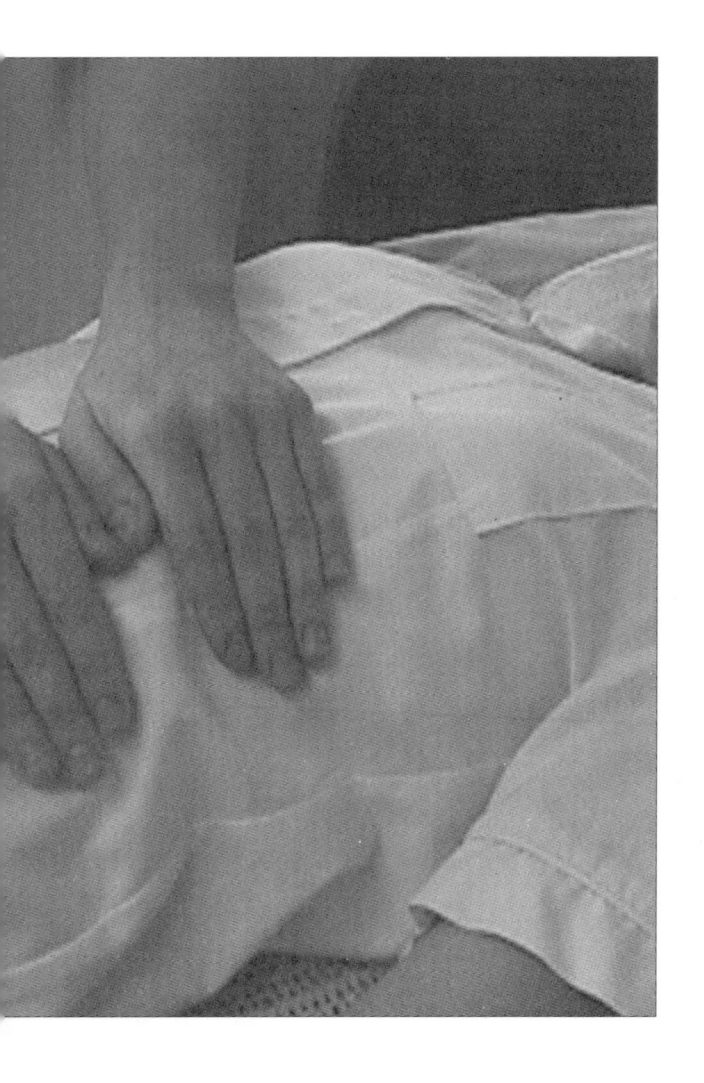

Third position is the Sacral Chakra, which governs the eurogenital system, reproductive organs and the kidneys are treated. The hands are placed in a line across the body.

In Chi Gung and T'ai Chi this area is called the TanTien, which houses vital energy. When this area is balanced one achieves a great sense of inner harmony and peace, as well as a feeling of self-worth. Desire in all its forms begins here, so when all is well in the Sacral Chakra it feels as if all is well with the world.

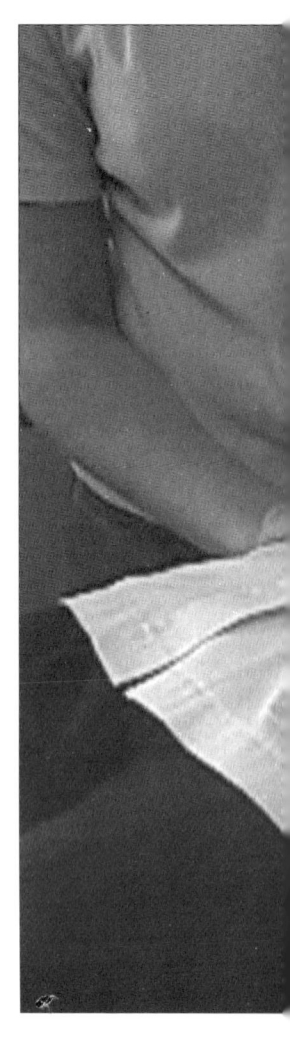

Treatment for others

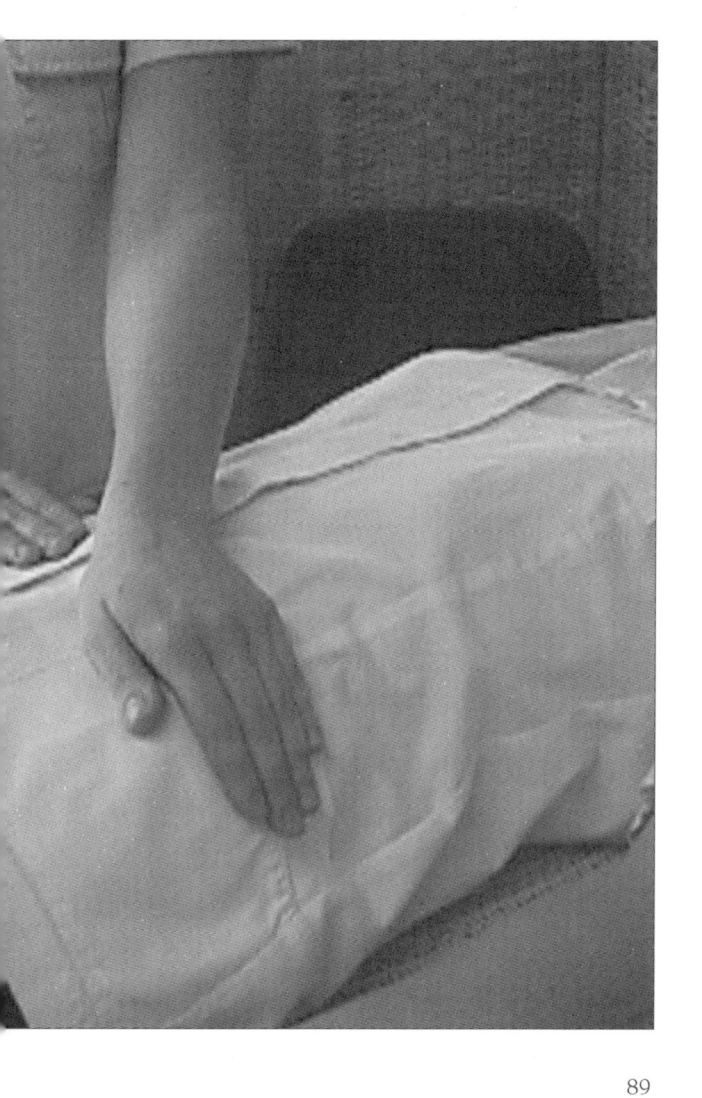

Fourth Position

Turn the hands, one up one downwards. This covers the Root Chakra and the genitals bladder and adrenals. This Chakra connects us with the earth and the natural instincts of survival and procreation.

Physical ailments profiting from this exercise include those of the sexual organs, appendix and eliminative system as well as lower back problems.

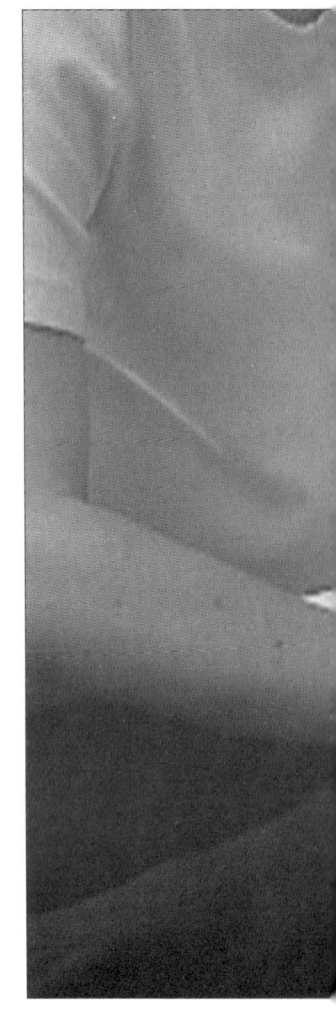

Treatment for others

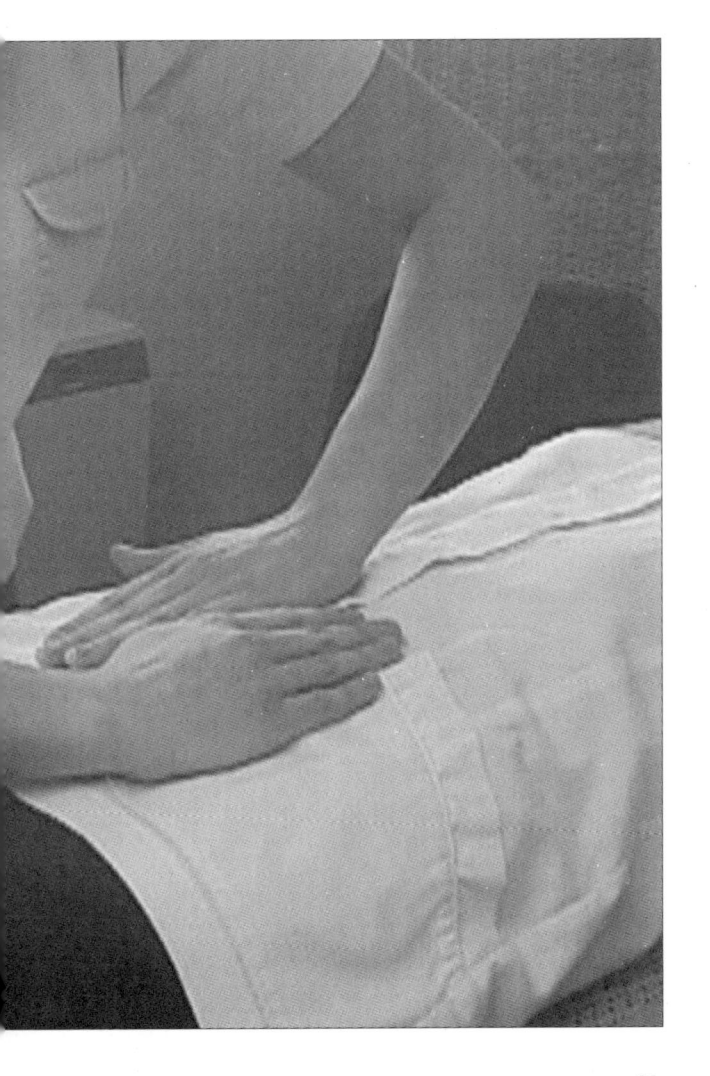

As stated previously, knee, ankle and foot positions are not a part of the traditional Reiki System but are to be recommended for establishing the greatest benefits from a session.

In the first leg position place both hands on the front of the thigh, just below the hip. Repeat on the other side.

Treatment for others

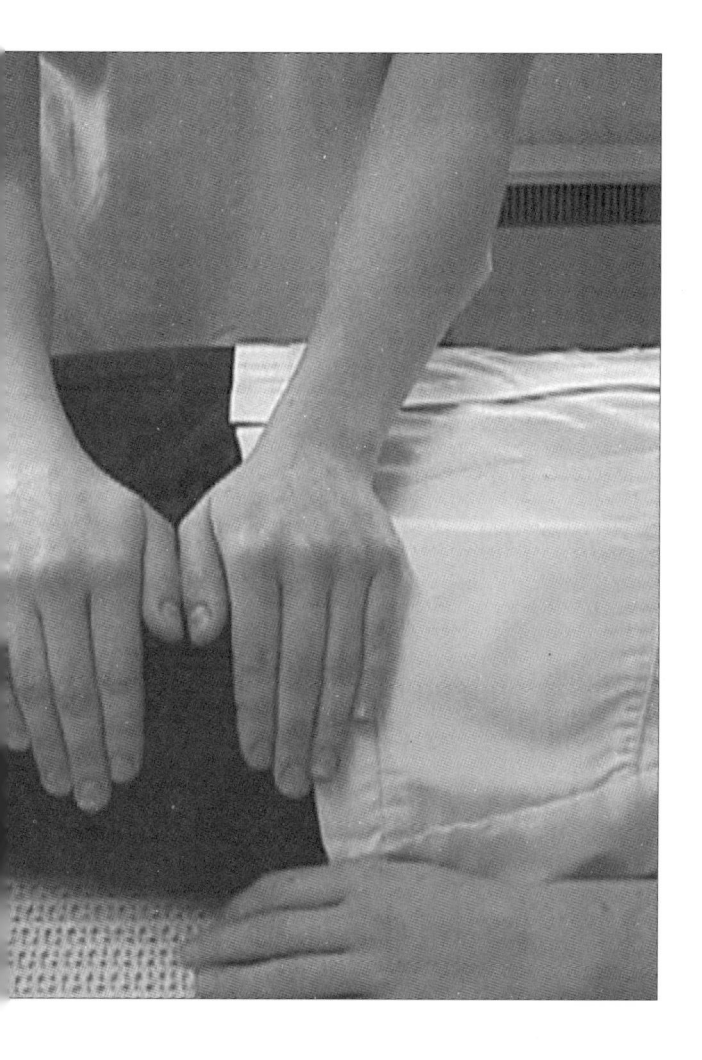

Second leg position covers both knees at once. Hold for about three to five minutes.

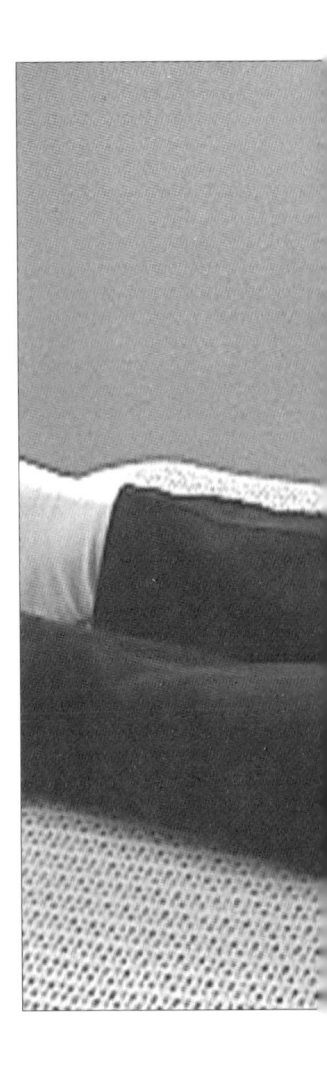

Treatment for others

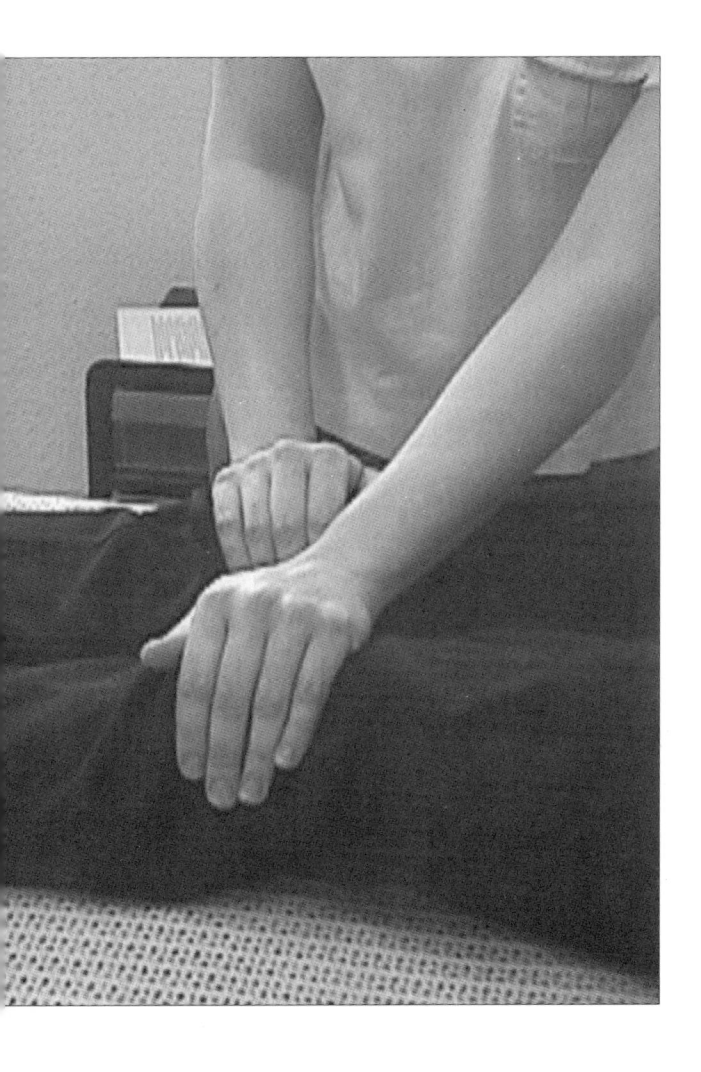

Next place the hands on the calves, one leg then the other.

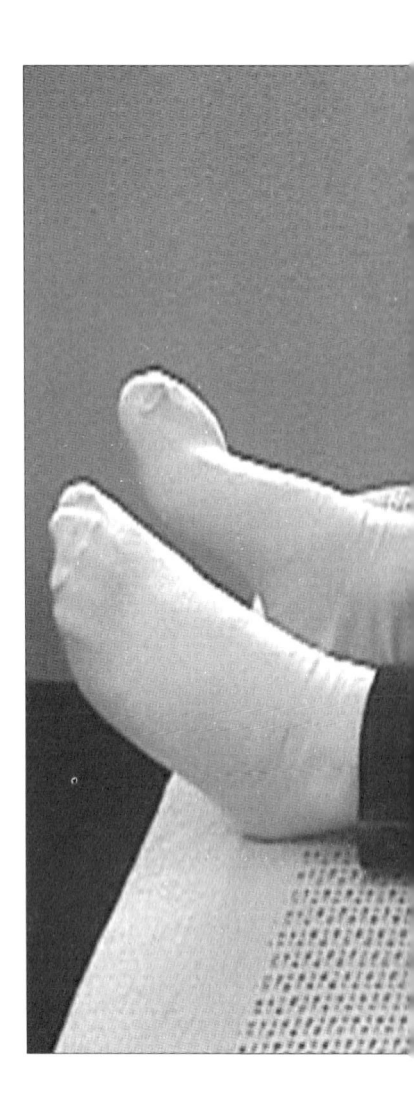

Treatment for others

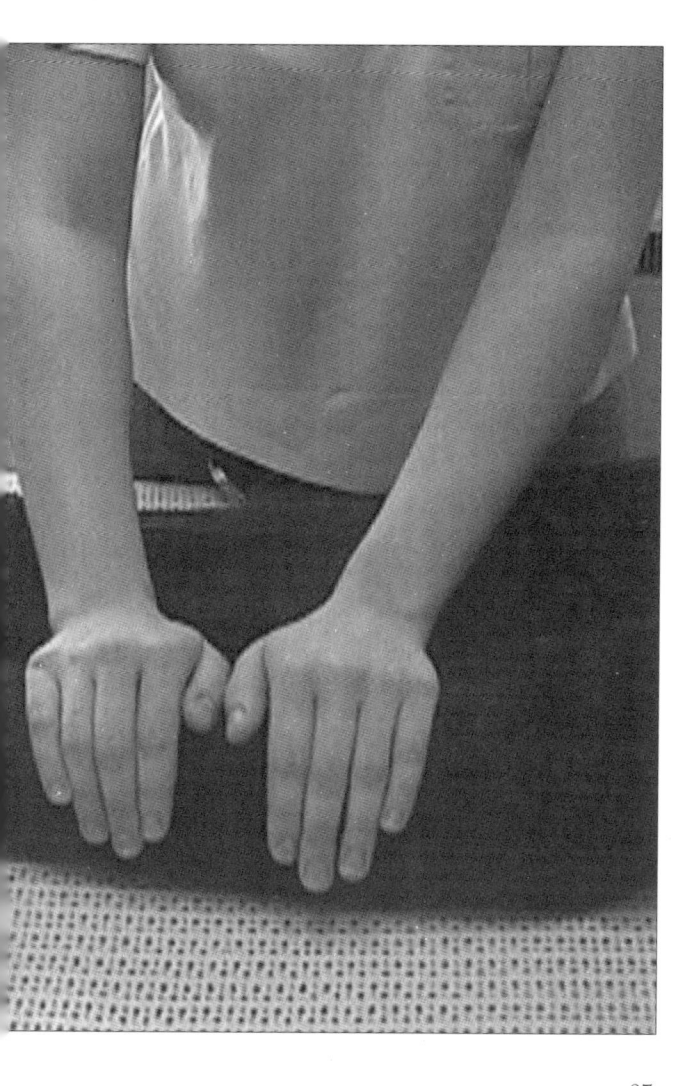

In this next position we can cover both ankles together.

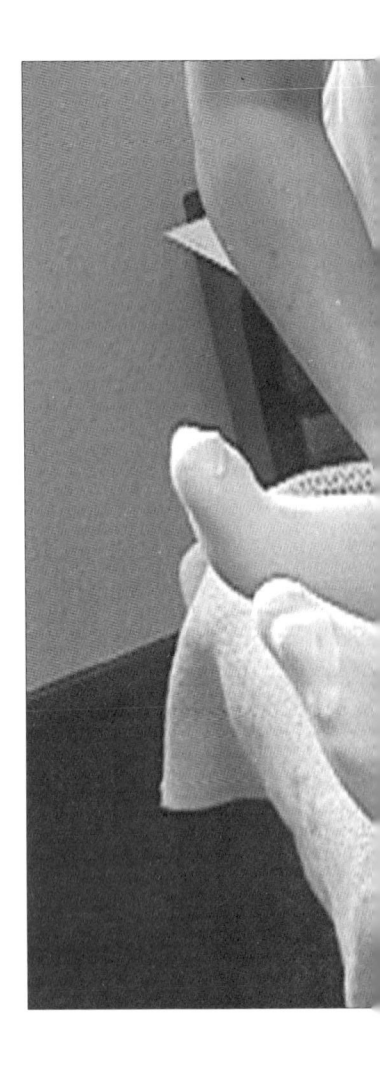

Treatment for others

In the next position, place one hand under the sole, fingers pointing toward the heel. The other hand is placed across the instep. Do the same with the other foot.

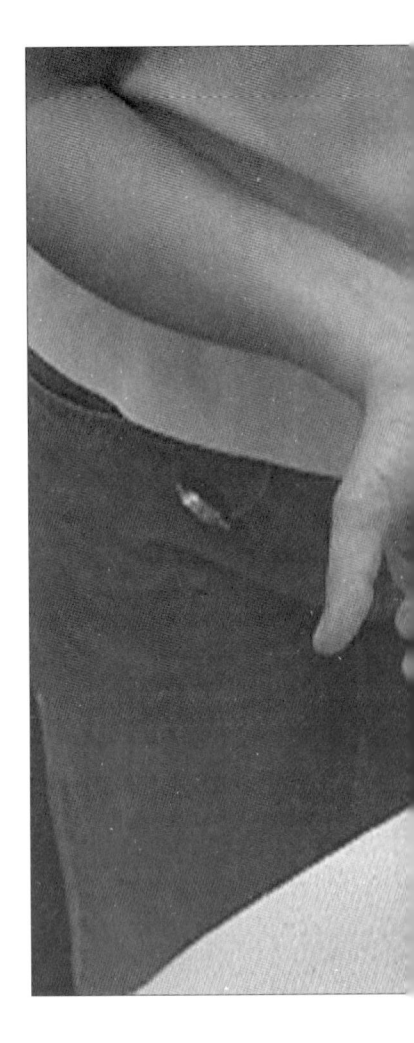

Treatment for others

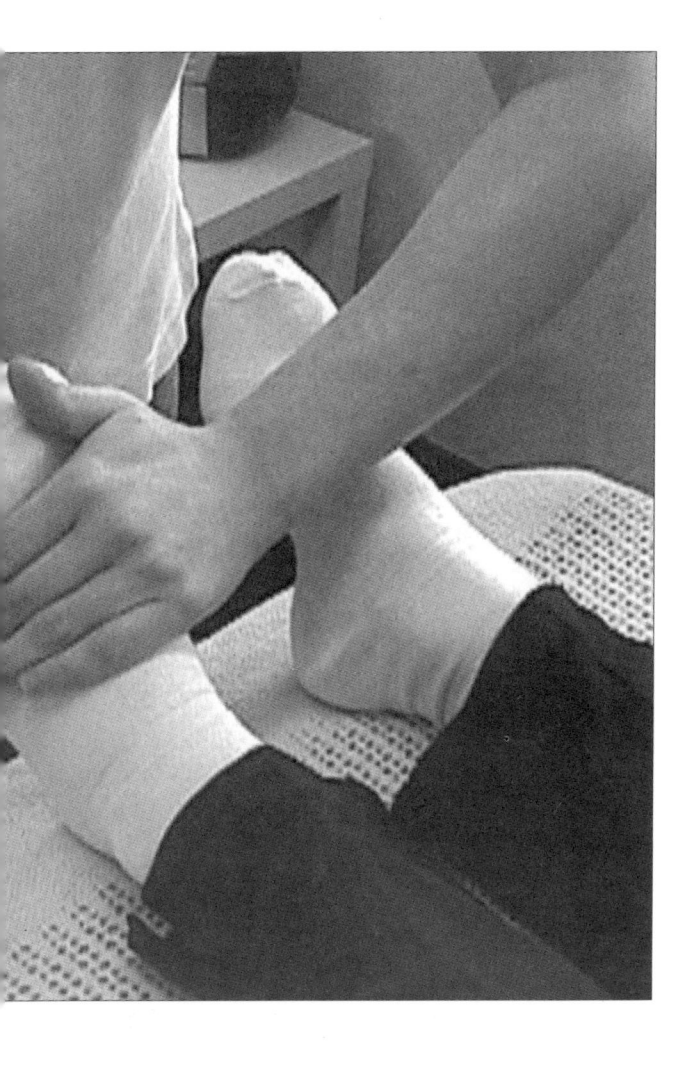

First position Back

Place both hands on the shoulder muscles at each side of the spine. These muscles suffer from excesses of tension, which result from body posture or internal reasons such as anger or stress. Either way you might need to spend more time in this area. The only way you will know is by listening to your hands. As they become adept at doing the work prescribed by the Universal Energy, they will tell you when it is time to move to the next position.

Body posture tells us a lot about a person, suggesting that reactions to life are expressed in this way. Problems in this area suggest an inability to let go. So be aware of your patient's reaction as the tension they are so used to, begin to diminish.

Treatment for others

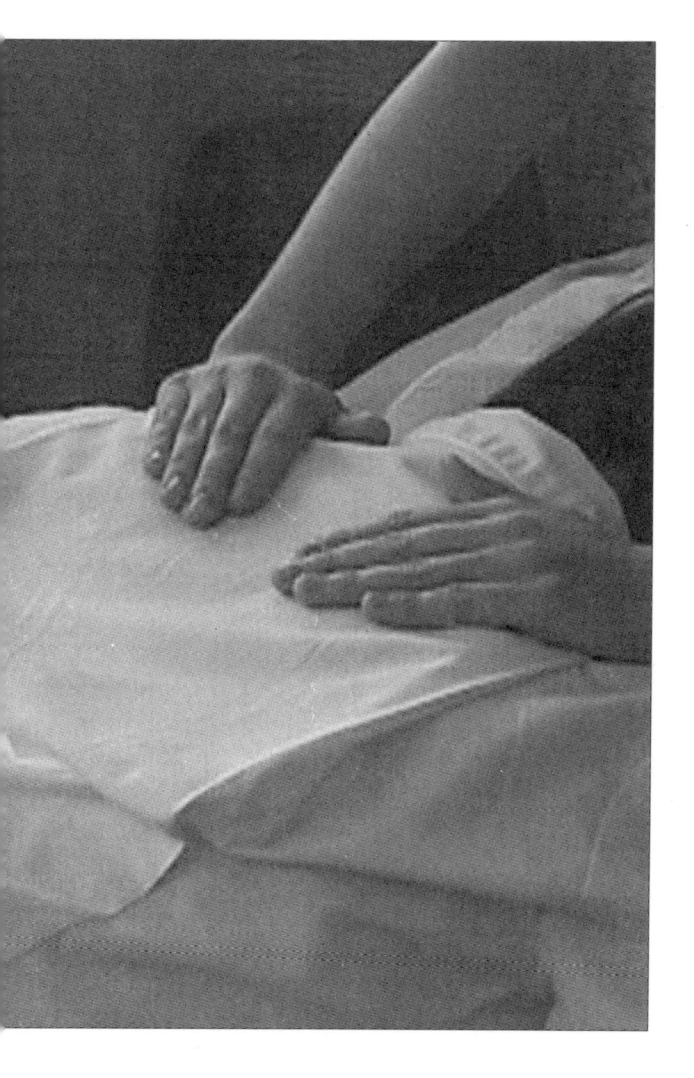

Second position Back

This is the back position for the Heart Chakra. The hands slide down together on one side of the back, in the area of the shoulder blades. The lungs and heart benefit the most; consequently complaints associated with these areas are treated directly. Emotional tension affects this area, resulting in depression and rage. It is necessary that one should be aware of the patients reactions should these surface. Explaining that the end result is a purging of these negative traits, ought to strengthen the recipients resolve to continue.

Repeat other side.

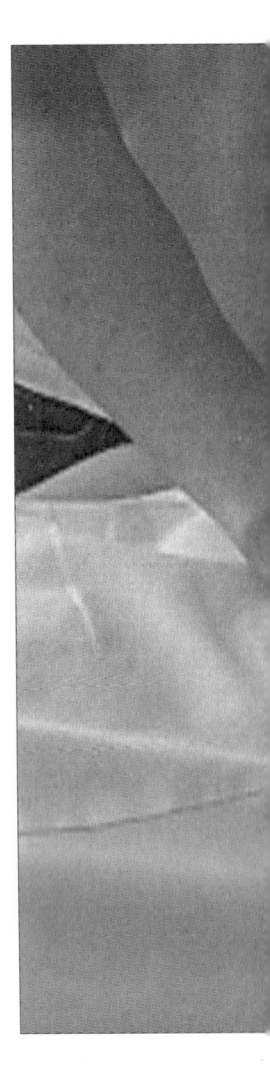

Treatment for others

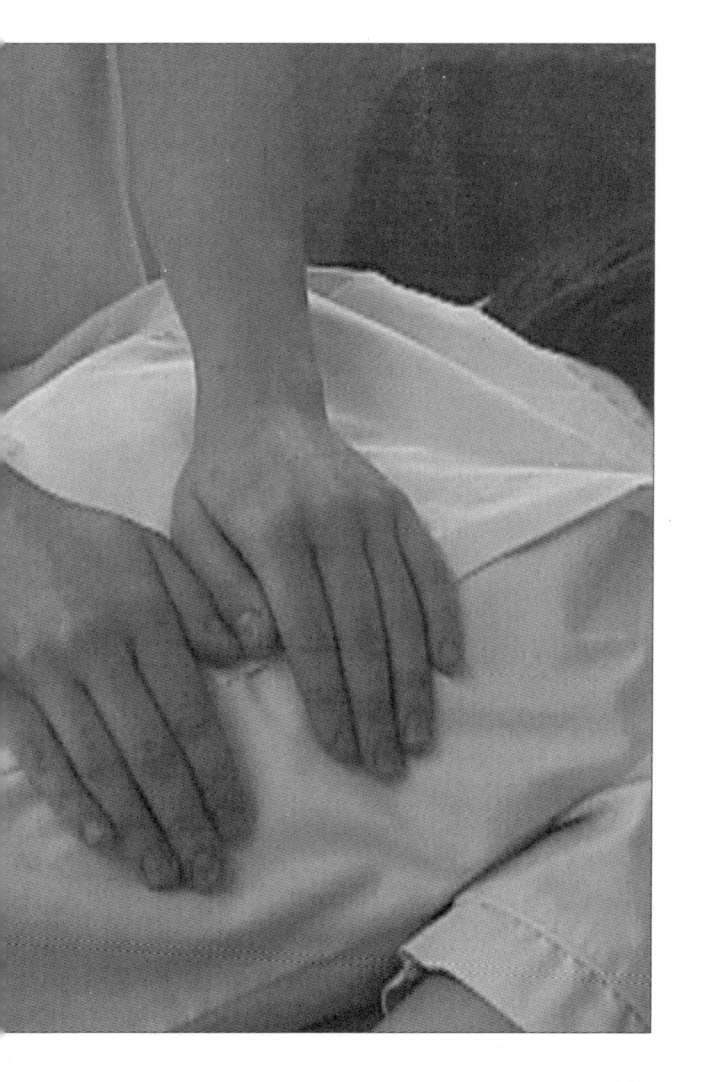

Third position Back

Placing the hands in a line across the body, move them down until they cover the kidneys. As with the front position, the adrenals also benefit from this position. Ailments associated with the middle back such as kidney disorders affect stature and well-being. Stress and emotional tension follow, so all of these disorders are treated from the Solar Plexus Chakra.

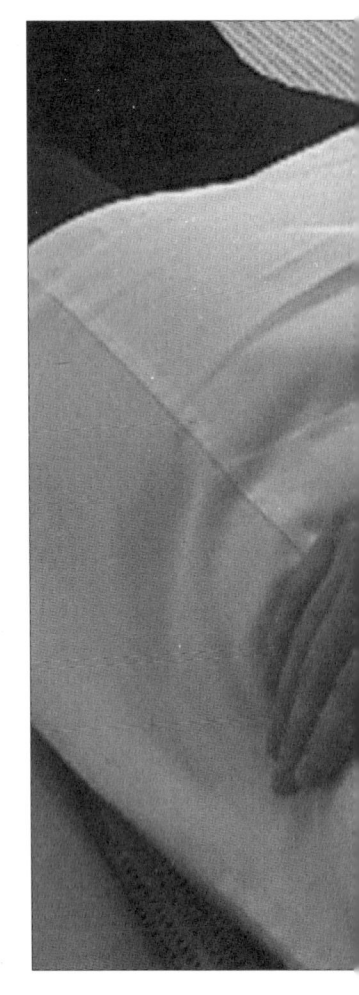

Treatment for others

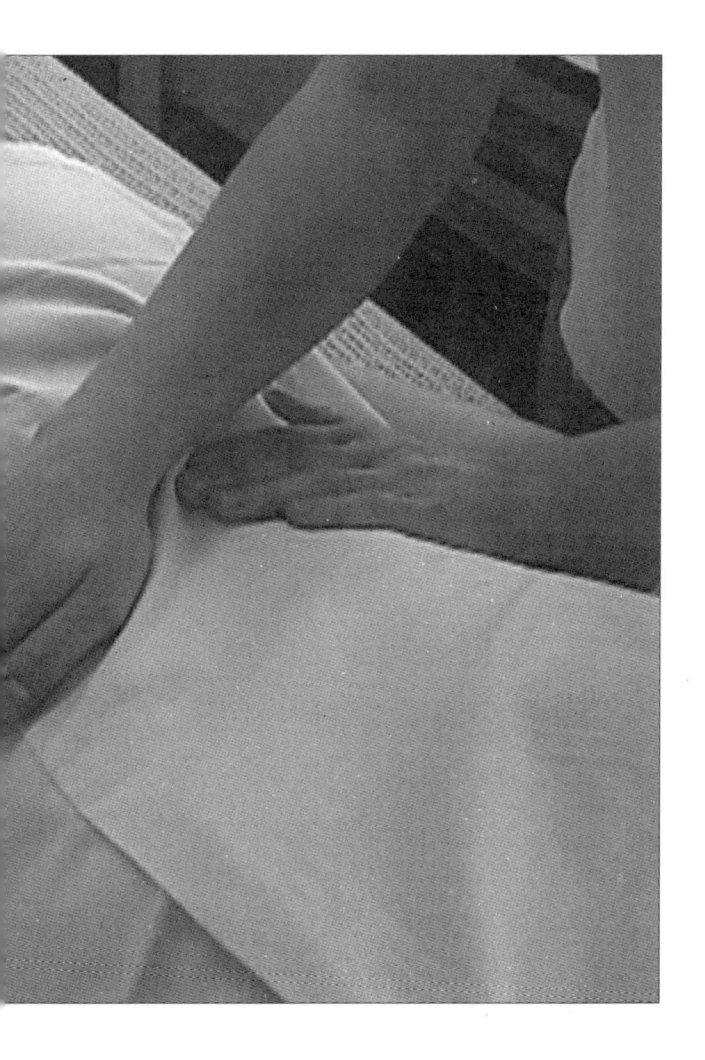

Fifth position Back

The final back position covers the sacrum. If one hand is placed crossways over the sacrum, the other hand is below it to form the letter 'T'.

This is the Root Chakra and its energy controls the small intestine, the sex organs and prostate gland. These benefit directly from this Reiki position. Complaints such as inflammation, haemorrhoids and sexual problems can be treated, though this may take a number of sessions.

A different alignment places the fingers of the upper hand on the sacrum. This position enables the energy to pass along the spine to affect the whole of the nervous system. Occasionally the effects of this are said to be quite dramatic.

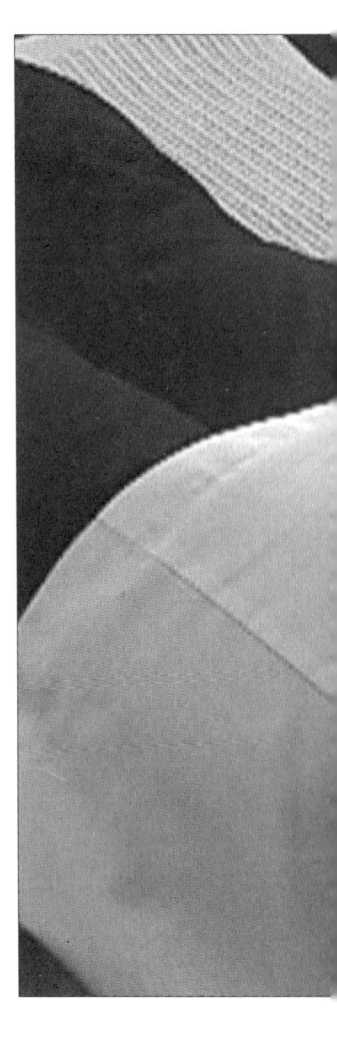

Treatment for others

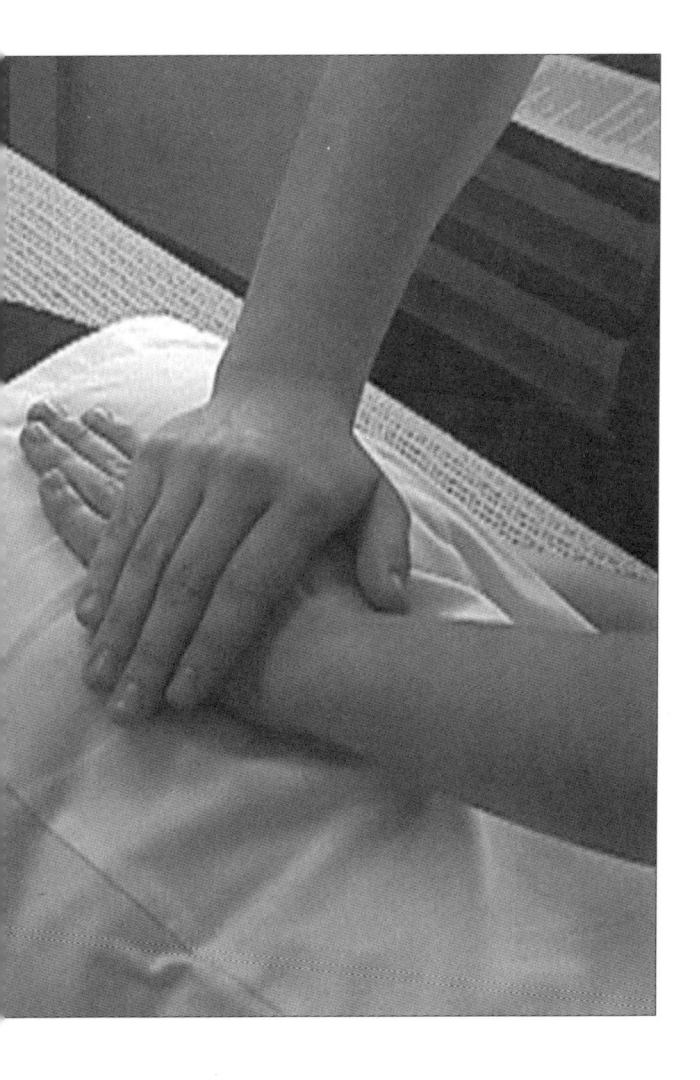

First leg position begins at the upper thigh, both hands side by side. Repeat for the other leg.

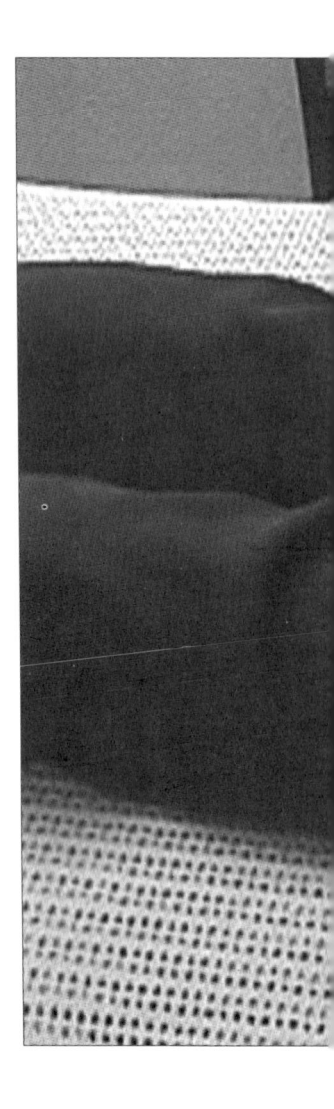

Treatment for others

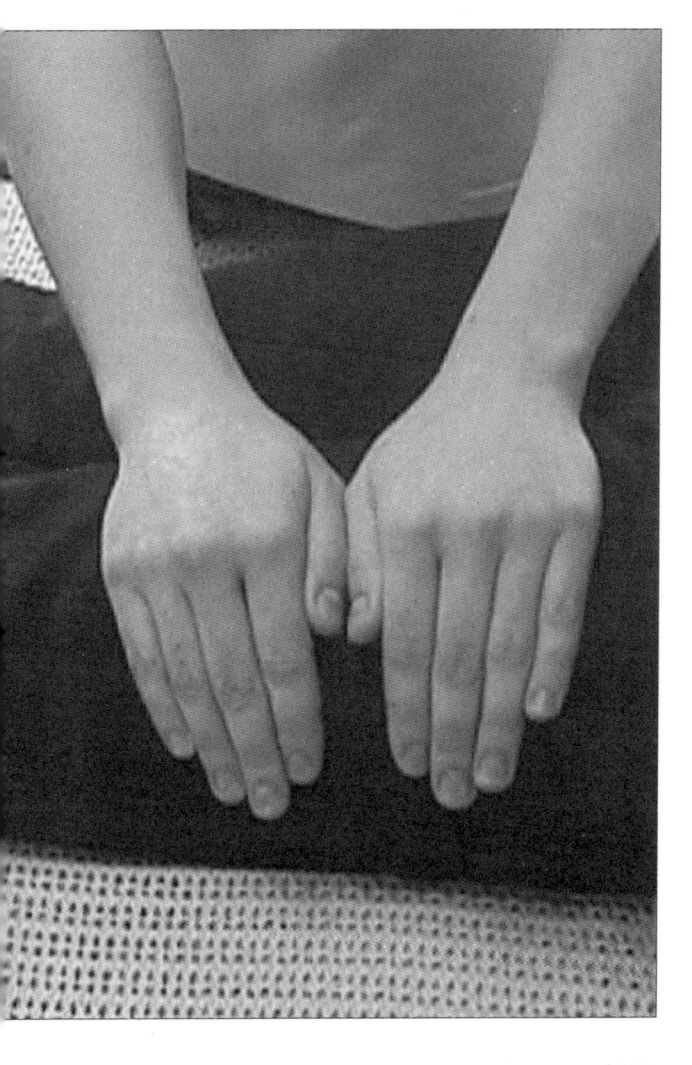

Understanding Reiki

Cover both knees together.

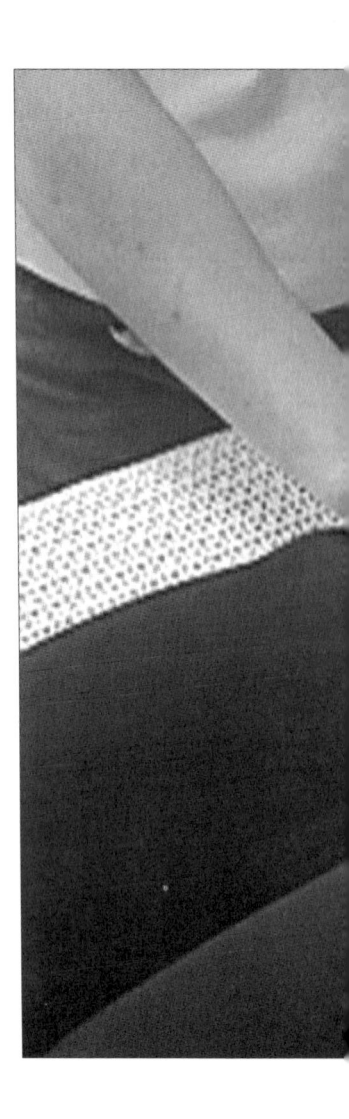

Treatment for others

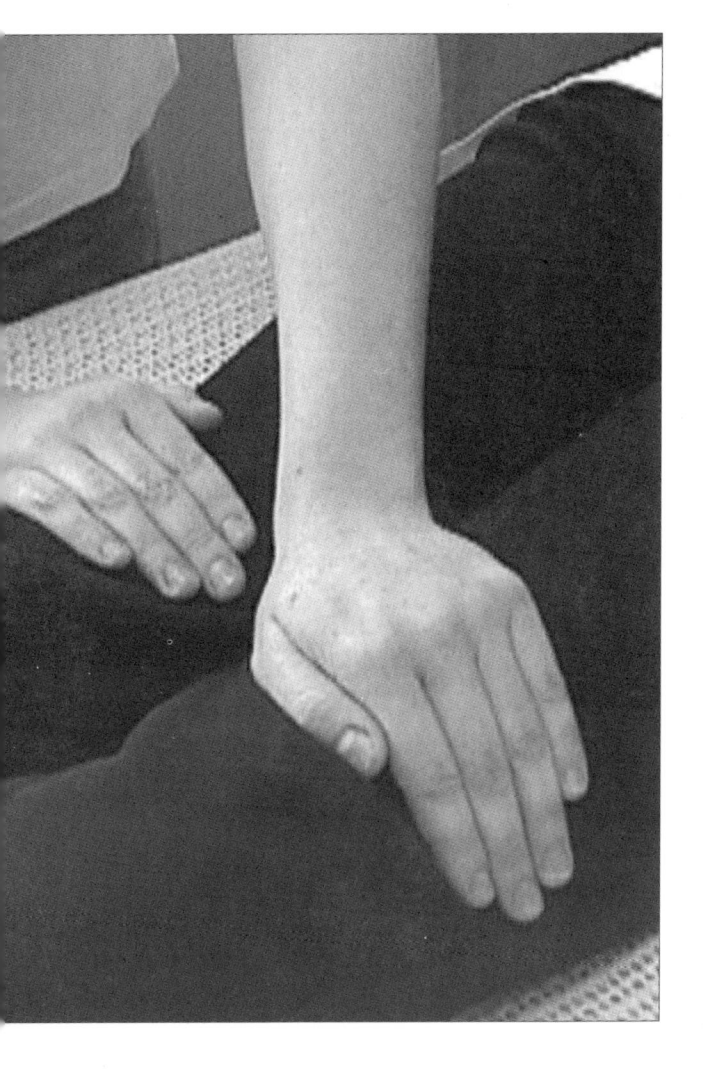

The calves are covered by both hands side by side, one leg at a time.

Treatment for others

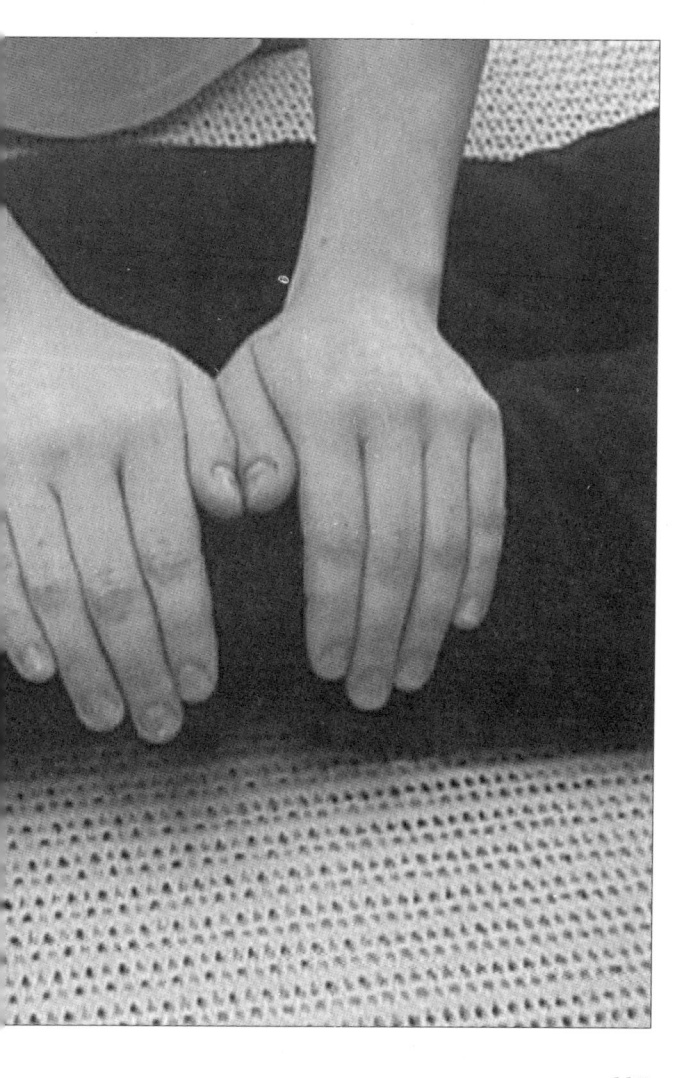

Ankles are covered together.

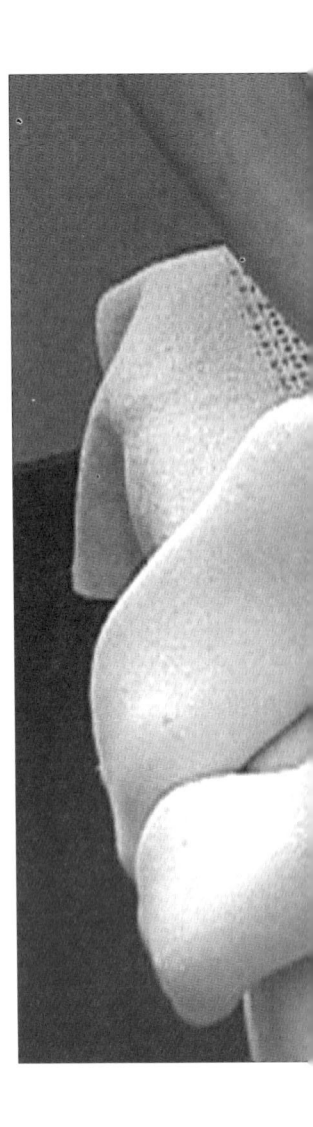

Treatment for others

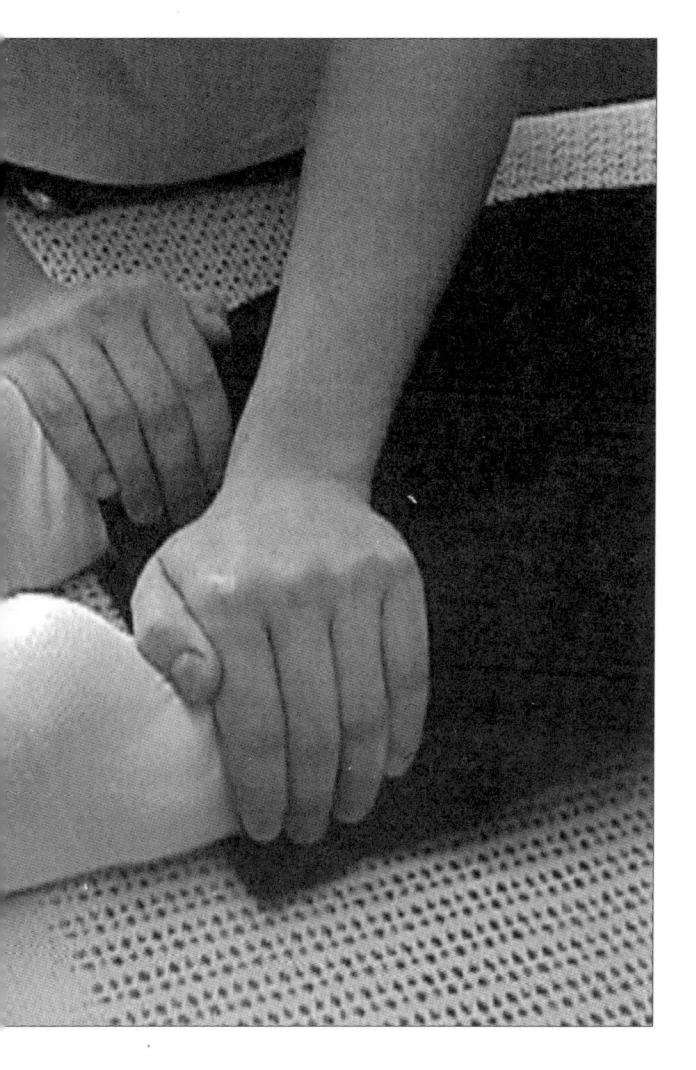

The final position covers both heels at once.

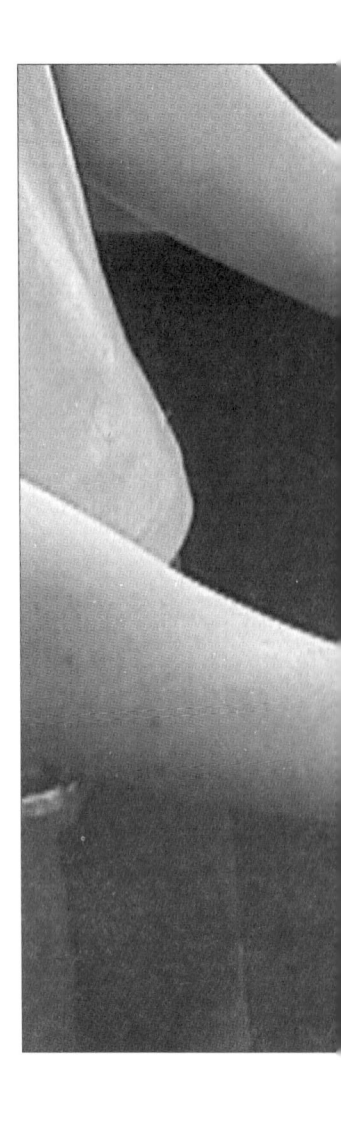

Treatment for others

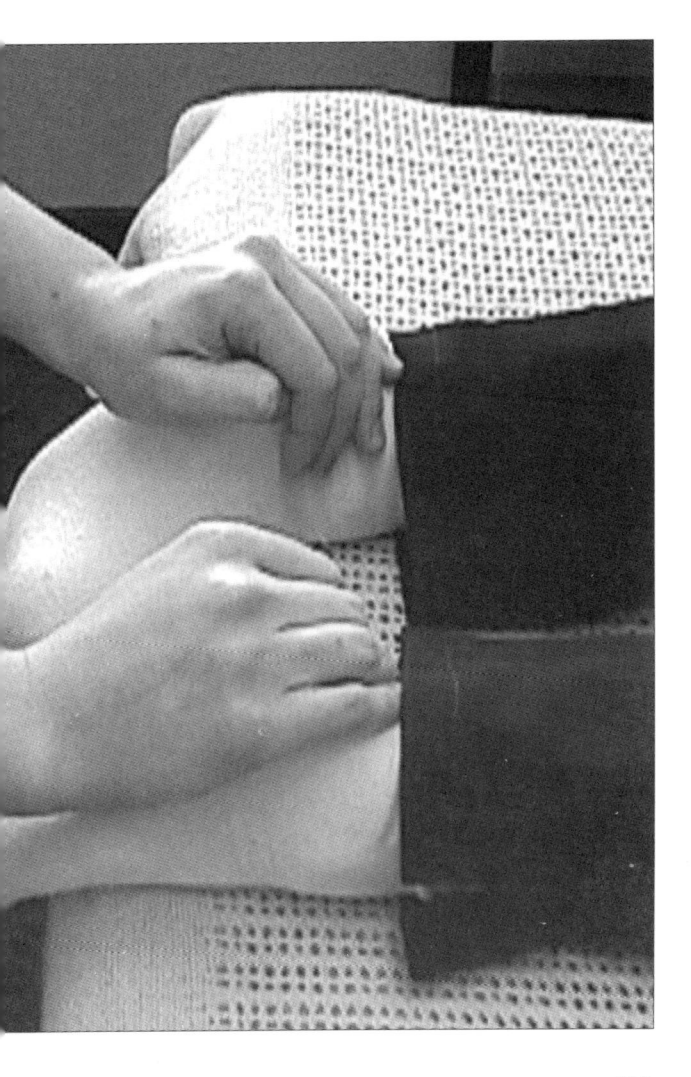

In T'ai Chi, even when standing for long periods of time, we allow the joints to stay open, almost as if we are *sinking* straight down through the joints.

(Read the chapter on Chi Gung concerned with *standing like a child*.)

When you place the hands on the feet of your patient you might find that they feel the movement of Ki throughout the body. The simplest position for this is to stand at the bottom of the table and to touch the heels of your palms to the balls of both feet. The primary benefit is to the Root Chakra, though the Sacral Chakra ought to benefit also.

This finishes the session and it remains only to perform a *grounding exercise*, and clear the recipient's aura.

Do this either by actually touching your patient or holding the hands a few inches above the physical body, but in their aura.

If you decide on the touching exercise place you hands on the outside of the hips, then draw down to the feet quite energetically. Next place the hands each side of the spine; press up to the shoulders and out to the hands. Repeat the above three times shaking the energy from the hands at the end of each movement.

If you prefer to work within the aura stand to the side of your patient; place the hands a few inches above the head and seep through the energy field to the shoulders. Move down and do the same from shoulders to hips and finally from hips to feet. Each movement ought to be repeated three times before moving on to the next step. Each should be energetic but relaxed.

After this we can leave the patient to readjust for a few moments, while we close down our own energy field.

Remembering the power and nature of the energies involved, our grounding ought to be in three stages. First we can symbolically wash our hands, then, repeat the principles as affirmations and finally perform a grounding exercise of our own. I have described the exercise that I use after a T'ai Chi or Reiki session, in the chapter about Chi gung.

Give your patient a glass of water and suggest that they move slowly and carefully, allowing their bodies to readjust. When the recipient is ready, and only if they feel safe to do so, we can discuss their reactions both during and after the session. It helps if we are able to do this without the patient feeling judged. If they are a little excited, we can be light and funny, helping them to express their mood. If they are serious or distressed, we ought to match their disposition with equal seriousness, in order that they feel free to discuss their concerns. Such an attitude strengthens the bond of trust between our new friend and us.

When we touch the recipient, we do so knowing that the healing energy goes directly to where it is needed, via the Chakras. We fully accept that it is accurate in a way that no human power can be. The moment that we attempt to enforce our will on it - we block it off. This is not an energy that we can harness; we can only open ourselves to it, allowing it to perform its natural function.

For this reason I have attempted to keep to a practical approach, neither labouring the scientific or metaphysical viewpoint. If something works, use it and seek an acceptable explanation for it later.

My descriptions of Chakras, which I have never seen, are the result of other peoples' investigations. My statements that certain problems arise within the human structure in a physical, psychological and emotional way, are also the result of the research of others.

My investigations begin after they have done their work. I find this to be practical way of working.

The question is always, 'Does it work?' If the answer is in the affirmative, and it might require more than one study, then use it and seek a fuller explanation later.

The Taoists claim that acupuncture, Chi Gung, Feng shui etc are all natural abilities: they have names and formula because the scientists of the day took time to study their realities. We may not agree with these names, or follow their formula in a traditional manner, but we surely must take note of their realities.

CHAPTER 5
Other types of healing sessions

Group healing

What is group treatment, and more importantly what is its purpose?

In a group session, more than one healer performs the healing. The recipient begins the session lying on their back. Each member of the group stands at different points around the patient. When the leader places his or her hands on the patient, everyone follows suit. Because of the number of healers, the positions are held for a shorter time, therefore each session is much quicker than one in which there is only one healer. Each then moves to the next position at the same time. There are more channels at work; therefore the energy is felt much more intensely.

One of the many benefits of this is that more patients can receive help. Alternatively, if the session is for the group only, there is time for each member to receive treatment.

Who can do the treatments?
Circumstances must vary according to the seriousness of the ailment, but generally speaking anyone who has Reiki One can take part. All of the group might have Reiki One only, but it is preferable to begin such a group with someone who has experience in this kind of work.

The healer, who stands at the head, ought to do all of the head positions. It is also more practical if this person both leads and observes the others. Practically speaking she or he is in the best position for this.

While to begin with the person at the head ought to be the most experienced, as the group becomes more proficient, this position ought to be practised by all of the others, as their confidence increases.

The number of healers will obviously vary, so at each session it wise to set out a plan or system. This system makes clear the responsibility of each of the healers. There can be nothing more discomforting, for your recipient, than having a group of people stumbling around in confusion. The situation might be highly amusing, and possibly in this way ice breaking, but not conducive to a relaxing session of Reiki.

Other types of healing sessions

The group as a whole feels a further and possibly more important benefit. Each is privileged to be a part of a single entity. While, as individual channels, we are aware of the intelligence of this healing energy, it is only as a part of a functioning organism that we begin to comprehend its spiritual nature.

As we observe the practical results of group healing, it becomes clear that the results have nothing to do with the human will, for if so, whose?

Another benefit is that as a group we can share our particular difficulties and understanding. Each of us observes and understands experience from a different point of view; this is our uniqueness. It stands to reason that as we share on a practical level, then our practical understanding broadens as a result.

Many practitioners of Reiki involve themselves in other forms of healing, and the philosophies behind these other forms. This is to be encouraged for many have direct and indirect connections with Reiki, while others are parallel. There are others also that use methods totally different from Reiki.

Western medicine, for instance, has an entirely different basis from most of their Eastern counterparts. All methods trace back to the same ideal however; to heal the sick. Whatever our opinion about this principle we will all agree, I think, that it is intelligent.

Our desire to heal might be selfish or altruistic, instinctive, intuitive or learned, but of one thing we can be sure – it makes sense.

It makes sense then to learn something of physiology; of psychology; spiritual healing and something about energy.

What is energy, indeed, what is intelligence?
We would not be looking for the terms, or an in depth knowledge of the content of these disciplines, only enough to insure an understanding that we can share or pass on to others.

As I have said, what we do in Reiki requires no analysis; the energy knows where to go.

I need to know something of illness to know when a cure is possible, miracles not withstanding. I am required to be of use to others before and after treatment; a fundamental part of disease is fear, and fear takes many forms.

If we are slaves to fear, then we are slaves to disease. The way to freedom begins with the knowledge and acceptance of this simple fact.

Other types of healing sessions

Reiki sessions for animals

If you are reading this book from a sceptical point of view, this might sound an unlikely proposition. But it is no more implausible than healing a human being.

The primary purpose of the Reiki energy appears to be: to return what was perfect to its original condition. If we can believe this, and it does seem to be self evident, then the nature of the energy itself must be that it is perfect.

Again, I will say that this is a self-evident truth.

As I have stated earlier, the Taoists claim that the use of Chi for healing is a natural occurrence. If this is so, then it explains why animals appear to accept Reiki, and other natural forms of healing. Reiki healers who have pets tell me that their animals relax immediately when they are being treated. The effects are pretty much the same as with human patients.

Animals require regular visits to the vet and Reiki does not pretend to replace these, but what it can do is prepare them for what is often a traumatic experience. One of the more obvious effects- that of Reiki's calming influence on the patient- is no different for animals. It is beneficial to give Reiki again as soon after the visit as possible, especially if the animal has been anaesthetised.

We are speaking here only of the pets of Reiki healers, but there is no reason why one should not specialise in treating animals, if the healer feels that they have a calling. Some people have a great affinity with animals, which the animals appear to recognise, and this makes them excellent healers in this area.

Other types of healing sessions

Reiki sessions for children

For many reasons a Reiki session with a child will be completely different to that of an adult. Like animals they are immediately and comfortably receptive, but also like animals they will get up and leave when they have had enough.

If possible make it like a game, and spend much less time in each of the various positions. Removing long-term energy blockages in adults can take many sessions, but this is not so with children: their channels are still free of this kind of encumbrance.

If you press a child, animal or indeed an adult, to accept Reiki because you want them to, the session will be a failure. Reiki works of itself, not through the human will. Reiki works of itself, not through the human will. If your child is too energetic to sit still at all, wait till they are asleep and apply the Reiki positions through the blankets.

Further to this, if your children also want to become Reiki healers, there is no reason why this should not be so. There are many families whose members are all Reiki healers.

Older members of the family can also receive Reiki healing, though a full session might be too much for them.

If you enjoy the company of elderly people, why not visit some of the local community centres and offer some short sessions.

Chapter 6
Second Degree Healing

We have discussed some marvellous healing in the early chapters: marvellous but not necessarily miraculous.

In second-degree Reiki we are about speak of healing a recipient who is not present- who may be thousands of miles away. I will repeat again what I said in the opening chapter, you cannot learn Reiki from this, or any book. What I offer is a description, an opinion, and a place to start – or not to start. If you don't like my description, but you really do want to heal others, get hold of another book.

If you are a sceptic, good – scepticism is healthy. But if you are a sceptic who wants to heal through alternative therapies, then you have what we call a dilemma: cursed if you do, cursed if you don't. All I can suggest is that you keep your scepticism healthy, and be willing to drop it if you see some proof to the contrary. You don't have to believe, but you could be willing to believe. Then try a Reiki session or two.

As we are attuned for Reiki One the changes we experience are mostly on the physical level. It is true that many of our destructive emotional and mental habits are removed during this period, but it is generally where these affect our physical lives.

For instance major defects like resentment, that stand in the way of our enjoyment of life, lose their power, and more positive attitudes begin to replace them. This process requires a period of time to consummate the liberation process: three weeks seems to be the optimum.

This time is necessary in the majority of cases because few of us can let go of so much clutter in anything less. Also it is reckoned that each Chakra takes about three days to complete its re-attunement.

When we approach the taking of Reiki Two, we are making a decision to enter a kind of healing we can know nothing about. In this book and others you can read descriptions of this healing, but the terms used are incapable of giving a proper account.

This was so for Usui also: when he found the Tantra Lotus Sutra he could not use it. His mind-set was incapable of receiving the true meaning of the symbols. It was only when he had exhausted every normal human avenue of knowledge, and was willing to open up to the intelligent power itself, that full understanding came to him.

In the introduction to First Degree Reiki there were three attunements, but with Second Reiki there

Second Degree Healing

is only one. When the healer as a channel opens up to receive more Ki, the Chakras increase in power, and the intuitive and mystical capabilities begin to increase. What is happening now is that the healer is developing an entirely new viewpoint. This is both disconcerting and stimulating. As the energy balance alters within, it can often seem as if one holds two extreme points of view at once.

The student is introduced to the symbols and mantras, which they must now learn to work with. It is the use of these symbols that intensifies the energy vibration for healing at a distance.

The symbols, being the result of spiritual intuition, are therefore sacred and there is some ritual involved in the passing of these signs to new students. The student is shown how to draw them, both on paper and in the air. All paper drawings are burnt at the end of the attuning, and so the student is expected to memorise them.

For healing at a distance there is a Reiki exercise, which involves imaging. This imaging involves a mental construction of the person to whom you are sending the Reiki energy.

Practising this exercise requires an undisturbed moment in which to concentrate your image. This image might include any representation you have of the recipient. You may remember, for instance how they looked last time you saw them, or recall the smell of their favourite scent. You might only have a photograph with which to work, or even the sound of their voice alone. These are all useful for the imaging process. Above all you must have their permission.

This form of healing requires meditation, and by meditation I mean a state of inner calm. In the first months of practising Reiki Two you will need outer calm to achieve this. There are exercises such as the mental tense and relax exercise in the chapter on Chi Gung, but as you become stronger in Reiki Two this calmness will come to you automatically.

Find a quiet place where there is little or no noise, strong odours or light: a place where the atmosphere is comfortable and conducive to tranquillity: a place where you can achieve serenity. There are many aids including oils, candles and music, which might help you to relax. If you find something, which helps, use it.

It is now time to use the imaging exercise. Once you have established contact via imaging, the rest is simple. Imagine that you are filled with light, then, send beams of this light and positive healing thoughts to the recipient.

If you have not received direct permission to send distance healing to a person, as a part of your meditation, you can firstly send a request for this permission. The reply ought to come back fairly clearly, but if it comes back rather vague, then you can send the energy, including with it a petition that

Second Degree Healing

the healing force, if it is not required, moves on to something or someone willing to receive it.

Reiki Two enters into the mystical realm of healing. Here we begin to use the symbols- to despatch the energy and treat the disease of the recipient. The actual process takes only minutes, once meditation has become a natural part of your day. The result however is the same as a full Reiki session but much more amazing. If you are lucky enough to get feedback from your patients, you will receive all the proof you need that it works.

Something to be aware of though, is that the energy of Reiki Two deals with emotional and mental imbalances. Physical manifestations of these problems are healed also, but this level of healing goes much deeper.

Through the imbalance of our patient can make contact with the energy itself. We can make an application to be shown the problem. This is using the techniques of prayer and meditation in a practical manner. We can ask questions- 'Is the difficulty it centred in the mental or emotional plane?' 'Which Chakra has become imbalanced as a result?'

The answers will come to us if we are willing and patient. The more we see health were there was only disease and unhappiness, the more we see the results of Reiki energy altering other peoples lives for the better, the more we will want to take part in the healing which is called Reiki.

After the healing session is over return to your everyday life. Concern and worry are unnecessary. Though we may feel it a positive step to continue to think about our patient's problem, conversely it will prevent healing – our own. When we worry, it is we who are ill, and the energy cannot do its job. Worry is in fact the work of self-will, one of the major blocks to natural healing. It is therefore the work of the disease, to prevent healing occurring. Make an image of health for your patient, and know that the work is being carried out by the Reiki energy.

In all of the instances of healing we discussed for Reiki One, we could apply Reiki Two distance healing. Remember, the distance, near or far, does not matter. If we have many patients to look after and not enough time to give them all a full session, we can use Reiki Two.

This is another way to give Reiki to children. If the young patient is too energetic we can apply Distance Healing. The imaging technique will also apply to your own Reiki session.

The primary skill is of course in the imaging – and because it is your imaging, the scope and definition of your images depend entirely on you. There are no rules in this area; everyone has different attributes. What is essential is that you use the symbols.

The changes for the practitioner are likely to be extensive. Here, as I suggested for Reiki One, it is vital that we gain as much information from our

Second Degree Healing

adjustments to this extra energy, as well as our reactions to those adjustments.

As most of them will be on the level of the psyche, it makes sense to share our findings with our fellow healers. This is another good reason to work with a group. Reactions on this level, even to positive alterations in the psyche, can be more than we are able to deal with alone. It is also likely that our judgements concerning such changes will suspect. It will help therefore to listen to more objective assessments from our peers, and of course offer them when the difficulty is theirs.

Reiki for practical daily use

Disease takes many forms and expresses itself in many ways: these manifestations we call symptoms. The cures for disease also take many forms, though they all have at least one thing in common- this is that they all treat the specific ailment with a specific solution. This is how it should be, and of course this is the basis for modern medicine, Taoist and related healing methods.

Practical observation and, testing of method is the only sensible approach to the eradication of disease. This must be so whether the method is empirical or metaphysical.

'Does it work? How and why? Can it be depended upon to work in any circumstances?' Practical questions demanding definite answers.

It is the experience of Reiki practitioners that the self-healing treatments result in a reduction in stress levels, a greater immunity to common ailments and a relaxed outlook on life in general. On a deeper level there is a sense of harmony and well-being such as had not been previously known, or even imagined. Finally, for those following what is termed, a spiritual path, there is the certainty that they have found a positive method to aid in their self-development.

In martial arts we say that small practise means small results: the same is true for Reiki: daily practise opens the channels, strengthens the body's

Second Degree Healing

acceptance, and the mind's understanding.

Half an hour in the morning will alter your whole approach to the day – try it. If the day is demanding, take a break- treat your Solar Plexus Chakra for five minutes and see how the energy flows again. Try an evening session to help with sleep, or simply to relax.

Many incurable diseases of yesterday are controlled by a variety of modern methods such as medicine, psychiatry and psychology. So broad is our modern knowledge, concerning sickness and its cures, that no one person can know it all. Modern of course changes with time, and so we find out more and our skills improve. The Taoists were also modern in their time.

In the following chapters I have included a description of Taoist healing methods and philosophies, followed by a brief outline of other alternative therapies.

This is not intended as a comprehensive list or an in-depth study, only as a demonstration of the variety of methodologies in use today.

While the techniques and systems are sometimes vastly different to those of Reiki, the purpose i.e. that of restoring health, or preventing illness, through the free flow of the life force, is the same.

Chapter 7
Other theories and therapies

Chi Gung

Chi Gung is an ancient Chinese art and science, by which the practitioner develops and cultivates the life force (Chi) by effort and practise (Gung). Exercises are performed through sequential movements like those of T'ai Chi (soft Chi Gung), or Gung Fu forms (hard Chi Gung). They can be practised as single techniques, sitting or standing, lying down or as part of sex.

Chi Gung can be performed quietly as in meditation, or with the use of sound, as in a technique known as six healing sounds.

There are such a huge variety of systems, each with its own arsenal of techniques, that it would be impractical to attempt a comprehensive study of Chi Gung. Of primary importance, for the interested student, is finding a good teacher. As with Reiki, this is not as difficult as it used to be, though it is worth spending some time in research, both of the material and the teacher. Invest in one or two books on the subject (you might use one the excellent examples in the bibliography at the back of the book).

The original system was called Nei Gung, which means internal development through effort. These were predominantly meditational exercises, used by Taoist sage-kings (*see* chapter on I Ching), whose primary purpose was to increase spiritual understanding and power. The fact that these exercises also maintained and regained superior health, and improved fighting abilities, was secondary.

Some useful Chi Gung exercises

The following Chi Gung exercises are practised for a variety of purposes, all of which, as you would expect, relate to health.

Still standing stance

This first exercise both balances and awakens the Chi. This is the *still standing* stance, which is also known as, *standing like a child*. (Shan Shuang).

Stand with the feet about shoulder width apart, the weight is evenly distributed. Relax the knees and hips slightly so that the joints are *open*. It is not necessary to sink to a position where the stance becomes painful or uncomfortable.

Other theories and therapies

Raise the elbows until they are in line with the ribs and turned down, as if they were too heavy to lift. The forearms extend to the front with the hands turned slightly inward, wrists relaxed. Again the joints are thrown open. This is to aid the free flow of Chi, throughout the body.

The head is erect without the neck being stiff. Imagine that there is a cord from the ceiling to the crown of the head. This gives the body a feeling of being light and suspended.

The spine is straight, but relaxed. The shoulders are also relaxed, which allows the chest to sink. This in turn allows the centre of gravity to sink to the abdomen. Breathe gently from the lower stomach, the place known as the TanTien.

Finally close the eyes and allow the tongue to touch the roof of the mouth.

Standing this way for about fifteen minutes enables the unbalanced energies to sink to the TanTien, where they become balanced. If practised regularly, you will sense your inner tensions immediately, and release them.

This is an excellent way to start the day, especially if you have some Reiki sessions to perform, or if your day is likely to be stressful. The time can slowly be extended up to about half an hour, after which you can add any or all of the following exercises if you wish.

Other theories and therapies

The first exercise balances disturbed energies, whereas this next one awakens the Chi, allowing it to flow freely through the channels.

Opening Stance

Stand as in the Shan Shuang stance, feet shoulder width apart, but with both arms hanging at your side.

Other theories and therapies

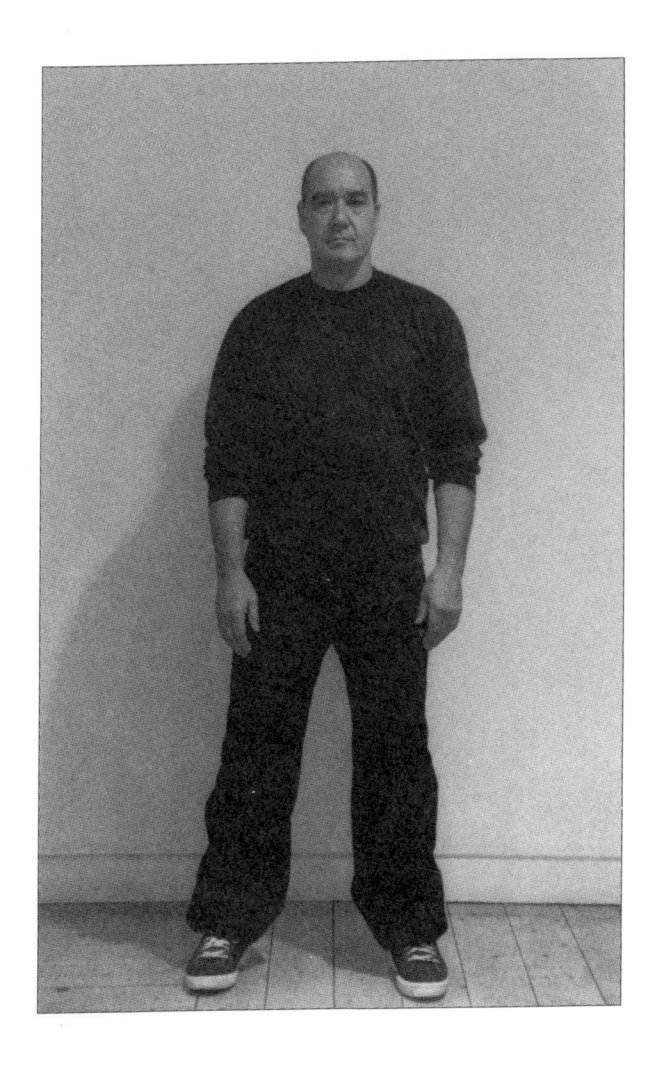

Relax shoulders and hips, then, allow both arms to float to shoulder level.

Other theories and therapies

The elbows point down and the wrists are relaxed. As the hands reach shoulder level, extend the hands and the Chi will rise to the fingers.

Other theories and therapies

Next let the shoulders relax, so that the elbows fall to the sides.

Now the elbows relax and finally the fingers. The hands are now at the sides again. Repeat the exercise twenty times. Hold the position for half a minute, between each repetition, to allow the Chi to settle in the TanTien.

During the exercise imagine you are in a swimming pool. Let the arms float up to shoulder level, breathing lightly into the TanTien, and as they float down, breathe out.

After a period of practise the fingers will tingle and the hands begin to get warm.

Other theories and therapies

Grounding exercise

The final exercise of this group can be used as a grounding exercise. It is a simple way of closing the doors after a session of Reiki or Chi Gung. This is the exercise I use after a T'ai Chi session. It is also the exercise I use after Reiki and I recommend it to other Reiki practitioners for the same purpose.

Use the shoulder width stance, with the arms hanging loosely at the sides.

Other theories and therapies

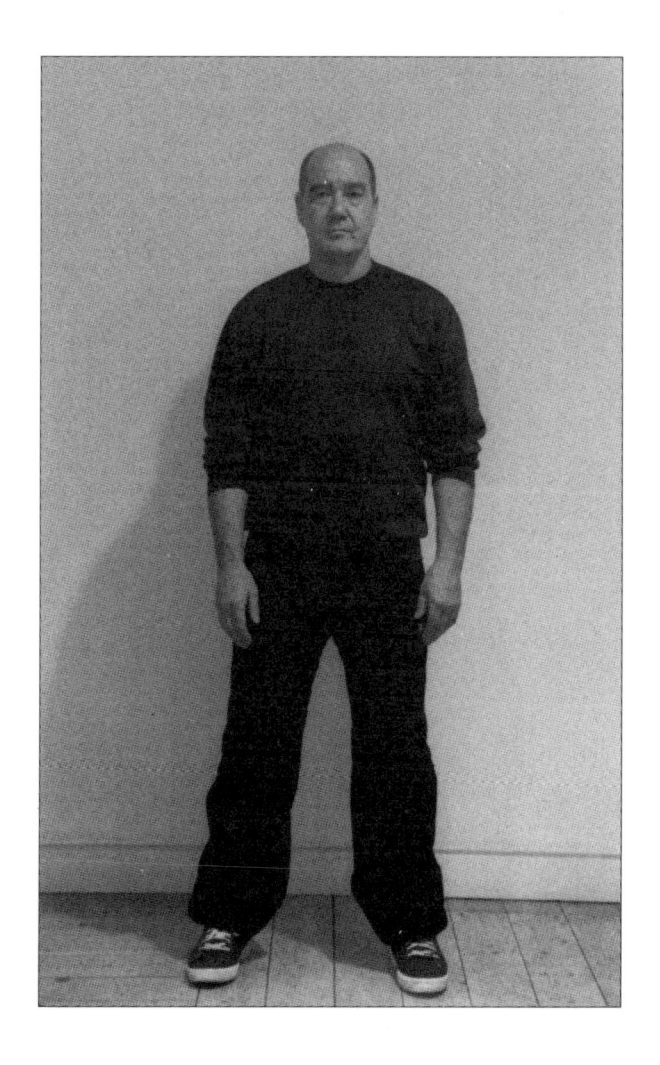

As you breathe in let the arms lift gently, stretched out to the sides, until they reach shoulder height, palms down.

Other theories and therapies

Continuing to breathe in, turn the palms over…

Other theories and therapies

...and bring them almost together above your head. This part of the movement is performed a little faster. As before the breathing is into the Tantien, or the lower abdomen.

Other theories and therapies

The elbows bend outwards, allowing the hands to sink to head height, then slowly down past the face and chest to the sides again, breathing out, but gently.

Other theories and therapies

Rest in the Still Standing Stance after each practise session.

Repeat the exercise for about twenty repetitions with ten seconds pause between each.

During the out breath of the above exercise, as the hands pass the face tell the muscles to relax. The same with the throat, chest, and solar plexus. Finally relax the abdomen, then the legs, all the way to the ground as the hands turn to the sides again.

With every repetition do the same with other parts of the body: so when we are at head height again, begin with the scalp, back of the neck, shoulders etc, relaxing the back as the hands fall past the chest and abdomen.

Once this is done, and you feel as if all the body is in a relaxed state, imagine closing the entrances to the Chakras, beginning of course with the Crown Chakra. The hands are in the position above the head and we are about to breathe out. As we allow the breath to leave and the hands sink to within an inch of the scalp, we concentrate on closing the door to the energy centre. Hold for about ten seconds before moving to the next point.

(The purpose of this part of the exercise is, as I have said, to close the doors. This is to prevent leakage of energy from these areas.)

Close the Chakras by telling them to close: in Chi Gung we are gaining conscious control of our energy input and output.

Other theories and therapies

After the Crown Chakra, move to the Brow Chakra. Concentrate, and then move to the Throat, Heart and Solar Plexus in the same way; finally the Sacral and Root Chakras. It will not be possible to close all of these Chakras in one movement: we will have to return to the opening position, breathing in again, then back to the head and down. Closing one at a time, then repeat the whole exercise to reach the next position, this works equally well.

Finally begin to close the back positions. Raising the hands to the head let them fall behind to the occipital ridge; then to the spine at a point between the shoulder blades. This last is a little uncomfortable at first but persevere with it.

Allowing the hands to fall to the sides, lift them behind the back to a place parallel, and a little lower, to the navel; move to the sacrum to finish.

In Chi Gung we have one more door to close, and this is at the perineum. Between the anus and genitals is the acupuncture point called the Hui Yin, and it is necessary to close this gate after practising Chi Gung. The closing exercise is simple and involves a contraction of the anus and genitals. This contraction is repeated three times, while concentrating on the closure.

The exercise in itself is finished and it remains only to relax for about a minute, while the Chi sinks to the TanTien.

As you can imagine, something formulated over

Other theories and therapies

thousands of years, cannot be learned in a day. This is true about Chi Gung; but it is only the knowledge involved in this discipline, which cannot be learned quickly.

Professor Zude Yee explained to me that the exercises we call Chi Gung, are observations of natural phenomena, made by generations of healers. These observations went through stringent tests, to prove their authenticity, before being passed on scrupulously.

Do not sit down immediately after Chi Gung exercises, stand in the still standing stance, this time with the hands at the sides, or walk around and perform light tasks. Do this for about five minutes, by which time the Chi will have settled.

Most important, however, is to find a good teacher. We cannot stress this enough.

TCM Traditional Chinese Medicine

As with the Ayurvedic tradition (see below), TCM is a holistic therapy. Amongst its vast array of health care practices is breath and movement techniques; herbal, diet and massage therapies, acupuncture, and acupressure and healing sound treatments. The list is extensive.

TCM is fundamentally shamanism, its principles being based on the philosophy of the I Ching and the sage-kings of antiquity. The interaction between the forces of heaven and earth, and man's ability to consciously use these forces, provide the basis for a system of self-development and health.

The energies are called yin (for earth), and yang (for heaven), and disease is seen as an imbalance between these two. These forces are relative, not absolute, and are in a constant state of flux: yang becoming yin and yin becoming yang. Because they are relative yin attracts yang and yang attracts yin.

Yin is perceived as the denser of the two energies, and links us to the world. Yin energy is expressed through food and drink, rest and the accumulation of energy. In a healthy way, yin allows us calm detachment from objects, in order that yang the primordial energy, can find expression in the world.

When the yin has become imbalanced, it is because we have become attached to the world, in a manner that blocks out the free passage of yang

Other theories and therapies

energy.

Yang, in everyday terms, is healthily expressed through ordinary activities, which benefit our society as a whole: the simple happiness we experience in helping others is an expression of yang in the world.

Yang becomes unhealthy when we are conscious of our actions and fall into the trap of observing self. In this condition we fall prey to habitual thought patterns and the demands that accompany them.

These demands manifest in many ways: overindulgence in food and drink, which quite often develops into the opposite as we become aware of the effects, and move from one extreme to the other, in an effort to control the excess.

We overspend or hoard money in the search for satisfaction; feed our vanities with ever-increasing demands on others and ourselves. The list is endless and encompasses the greatest proportion of human misery.

Health is similar, in TCM, to that of the Ayurvedic system: to be well, we need to be whole: to be whole means to know what we are made up of. A state of denial describes the insane and blind rejection of the true condition.

Sun Tsu in the Art of War tells us success depends on,

Knowing the enemy and knowing oneself;

Sometimes the most dangerous enemy is within self.

The I Ching separates the human mind and the mind of Tao, or Universal mind. This does not mean that they describe two disparate entities, only that they are dissimilar levels of the conscious mind, each having its own activity. Problems occur when one seeks to subjugate the other.

TCM is a practical system of health, a holistic system with a simple base: well-being occurs when yin is yin, and yang is yang. When the human mind, (yin) controls the Universal mind, (yang) imbalance (disease) is expressed in our whole being. And equally, when yang seeks to control the lower functions, misery occurs.

The primary purpose of TCM is prevention of disease, and only in a secondary sense is it viewed as a cure.

It is the interaction between the primary forces of Yin and Yang that results in change. Change is the path of development: comprehending and plotting this path leads to health.

In the evolutionary process of I Ching and TCM philosophy, the Chinese sages observed how the primary forces operated in the seasons.

In spring yang is present as vital energy, an awakening life force, overcoming the death-grip of winter. In summer, as yang reaches its zenith, in a flourish of energy, they detected the faintest movement of yin can be detected. Autumn is the unfolding of yin, and the withdrawing of yang.

Other theories and therapies

Finally, as the cold of winter prevails over the world, yin is in the ascendant.

Spring is dubbed young yang; summer old yang; autumn is young yin and winter old yin.

This was how the interaction of forces manifests to create change in the world.

Spring signifies the first outward movement, an expansion, while summer is an extension of energy, upward. In autumn there was a contraction, while winter entails a downward, resting movement. These movements occur about the world and so each is assigned a direction.

Spring outward to the east.

Summer up and to the south.

Autumn a sinking of energy and to the west.

Winter a downward movement to the north.

With earth at the centre, these became the five stages (movements) of change. (Often incorrectly called elements of change).

From these five stages, and their attributes, the Chinese sages generated an intricate methodology for combating disease.

The five phases were symbolised by earth, wood, fire, metal and water. The characteristics of the five symbols of change were then assigned to the five major organs, and the emotions that spring from them.

The organs produce, change and control the Chi (Ki, Universal energy), as well as the blood, via channels throughout the body. As regards the Chi, these channels are called meridians.

The sage healers concluded also that the spiritual aspect of the individual manifested through the organs, in a variety of ways. The word for spirit in Chinese is shen, which can be singular or plural. Singularly it is the spirit governing the heart, whereas in a collective sense it represents the spiritual aspects of all of the organs.

This can seem quite confusing, but if we take it to signify spiritual qualities, rather than entities, we can apprehend the meaning more easily.

Taoist healers observed that when the quality of spirit was strong, the body, thought patterns and emotions were both healthy and strong.

In conclusion, the primary purpose of TCM is to achieve balance of the primal energies, preferably before the onset of disease. This is the simplicity of its methodology. This straightforward approach is evident in all avenues of TCM, i.e. herbal, T'ai Chi, acupuncture or dietary.

In the I Ching, self-development is the work of the character, or higher self. Correct practise of T'ai Chi Chuan has equivalent aims. This indicates the intention of Reiki, Chi Gung, T'ai Chi etc. Intention, in this way represents the will of the intelligent energy, as directed through the attributes of character (higher self).

Other theories and therapies

T'ai Chi Chuan

T'ai Chi Chuan is currently performed, primarily, for its martial and health aspects, although it is achieving respect for its purely callisthenics qualities. It is known as an internal martial art, because of its emphasis on the development of Chi, as opposed to muscular training.

As with Chi Gung, with which there is a direct connection, the movements concentrate energy on the organs and systems of the body. The Chi is encouraged to flow more readily through the channels, (or meridians) to ensure a balanced system. Opening the joints and cavities of the body allows this free flow of energy through the many channels: the three most important of these pathways are the left, right and central channels. All three channels occur in the centre, i.e. mid point between the front and back of the body. The central channel joins the left and right channels at the crown of the head, at the extremities of the fingers and toes, armpits and the area around the hip-bones.

Other significant channels are the yin and yang meridians. Yin channels pass along the front of the body and the insides of the arms and legs, while the yang channels are on the outside of the arms and legs and up the back. Jing lo channels direct the flow of Chi around the trunk, in a series of connective belts.

In the practise of T'ai Chi Chuan, the first

emphasis is on the external forms. There are many reasons for this: for instance the free flow of internal energy depends on physical co-ordination. More importantly however, is the part that the conscious mind must play: the mind must control the movements from the centre. This centre is located just below the navel, and so awareness must be there. This exercise requires constant practise before proficiency is achieved, but once it is, all of our activities begin to take on a new and harmonious significance.

The centre and consciousness must attempt to become one: to move in unison but the lower centre guided by the upper centre. This principle originates in the I Ching: the second and fifth lines symbolise centres in the upper and lower trigrams: for there to be natural balance, the higher self must direct the lower self, but only from a position of unity.

The lower centre is yin and therefore relates to the earth: we encourage this by sinking. This is done by relaxing the muscles and allowing the joints to move freely: this in turn allows more energy to circulate through the various channels: blood, breath and Chi sink toward the earth, providing relaxed power at the centre. The principle we call sinking might also be termed grounding, in that, we are consciously aligning ourselves with the force of gravity. Strange as this might sound, once we have become accustomed to this we find we are far more relaxed mentally and

Other theories and therapies

emotionally. This is because we are no longer pressing ourselves away from the ground.

The body is aligned in a particular way: the head supported by the spine, the spine by the pelvic girdle, then through the legs to the feet, which support everything.

In T'ai Chi, learning to carry the body this way with the joints relaxed and open, breath sunk into the centre, creates a wonderful sense of well-being.

Once the consciousness enters into the centre and we achieve a sense of harmony, we begin to recognise the difference between responding and reacting.

When the lower centre moves without the control of the upper centre i.e. the conscious mind, this is called a reaction. An objective mind responds calmly and clearly to a given situation: the speed of response depends entirely on the situation (see Chian Long Classic below).

When the lower centre directs movement, in a reactionary way, it is the instincts that are directing it. This is explained in the I Ching in the following way: the third line, symbolising our desires, emotional reactions or instincts, presses down and seeks to control the lower functions, (symbolised by the two lower lines) by blocking energy from the fifth line. The imbalance created by this causes disease and lack of harmony in the whole structure- creating fear, the need for more control, and so on.

With practise we begin to understand that the

energy of Chi (Prana, Ki or Life force) is as immediate as our thoughts. When the conscious mind and the body are correctly attuned (i.e. to the present moment), all of our activities are filled with a vitality and resonance we have not experienced since childhood.

Practising forms at such a slow pace requires great discipline of mind to begin with: learning the principles of movement, balance and relaxation, as well as co-ordinating emptiness and fullness can be extremely demanding. Each time the form is practised the mind is continuously alert for areas requiring improvement: this also includes negative reactions such as impatience and boredom.

After the forms have been mastered, the internal energy begins to pass through the body and limbs as a result of the conscious will. As the physical co-ordination improves, channelling the energy from the heels through the waist to the upper limbs becomes effortless.

It is important, in T'ai Chi training, to learn the method (forms) as well as the principles, but if we focus on one at the expense of the other, our practise will be meaningless.

In Chen style T'ai Chi this imperative is no more important than in learning the Chan Si Gung, or Silk Reeling method. This method of movement, and the inner force produced during the practise of it, can only be mastered when we can adequately apply the

Other theories and therapies

principle of sinking to all the joints, and consciously direct all movements from the centre.

In T'ai Chi terms, employing yin means to make oneself empty, whereas yang means making oneself full: yin is gentleness, yang is forcefulness.

T'ai Chi Chuan Classic of the Chian-Long Dynasty (1736–1796)

Chang San Feng is one of those credited with creation of T'ai Chi Chuan, and it was he who wrote the original treatise in the Song dynasty (960–1127 AD). Many masters of the art have formulated their own account of this text and the above named classic is one of them.

In translating ancient T'ai Chi texts we are met with two difficulties. Firstly the scope of its philosophy is so vast: at one extreme T'ai Chi, viewed in its simple form is a slow dance; while in its more complex and esoteric extreme it is representative of the evolution of the Cosmos. (On the one hand structure, on the other meaning.)

The second difficulty is simpler and arises out of changes in writing style in the past 200 years. As with all languages, alterations in Chinese have occurred as a result of the advancement of culture, and so it is with no surprise that we can observe vast differences in the numerous translations.

In the family tradition of Professor Zude Ye, the practise of T'ai Chi is really quite simple: play it like a slow dance. The more you train, the more you will want to train, and the more you will understand how and why you train.

The theory in the Classic of the Chian Long Dynasty appears to be in the form of a map, which

Other theories and therapies

prepares the newcomer by offering simple guidance. If you have the map there is no need to remember as a result of study, simply use it to check your movements each time you train. You will assimilate it with practise.

The following is the translation with amendments, by Professor Zude Ye, of the T'ai Chi Classic of the Chian Long Dynasty. I offer this to show the reader the simple view, concerning the movement of Chi, in the original texts.

- For the Chi to move along the neck to the crown of the head it is essential to relax the shoulders.
- The Chi then sinks to the Tan Tien (lower abdomen) and is guided along the thighs and hips.
- The *Ha* sound emitted from the Tan Tien extends the Jing (energy), strengthening the fists.
- The five toes grasp the ground; the back (top of the body) is bent like a bow.

(The following teaches about *still standing* posture.)
- Inhale to Tan Tien.
- Transfer Chi to sacrum, then up to crown via the neck;
- then down front of body to thighs, lower legs and toes.

- The *still standing* posture of T'ai Chi is the basic for a firm stance and the free flow of the Chi.

- During motion be light and agile and condense the spirit hidden within (the whole body).
- Move continuously so that the Chi flows steadily.
- When the intention is to move to the right, the first movement is to the left and vice versa.
- If the movement is up then the intention is to first go down; again the reverse applies.

- To refine the internal Gung Fu the key is in the Tan Tien.
- Hin and Ha the two Chi's are infinite.
- Chi separates to yin and yang in movement and unites in stillness.
- Follow your opponent, if he extends you bend- or the reverse. Slow responds to slow, fast to fast.
- These principles must be thoroughly understood.

- Suddenly appear or disappear, moving forward but no more than an inch.
- Regarding balance, even one feather added may break it and the Tao is hidden within it.
- Hands move slow or fast depending on the situation.

Other theories and therapies

- When this principle is practised and understood four ounces can deflect a thousand pounds.

(The next two parts are strategies for combat.)
- Be prepared for changes.
- Whether forward back left or right do not move to excess; the key is balance.
- Speed depends on the opponent; borrow his force to defeat him.
- Hen sound comes from the lungs and links with the nose; ha sound comes from the stomach and links with the mouth.

- Wardoff, rollback, press and push are the primary directions.
- Pluck, split, elbow and shoulder are the four corners.
- There are eight kua, or trigrams, corresponding to the I Ching, which are kan, k'un, chen, sun, chien, tui, ken, and li.
- Forward, back left, right, rear and centre represent the five elements.

- Extremely soft means hardness: like a needle hidden within cotton.
- Move as if drawing silk but be clear about your

direction.
- Open and extending, tight and compact one upon the other; movements should be threaded together tightly.
- When there is an opportunity for action move like the cat.

(And so the strategies for action are:)
- Hard is to be found in softness like a needle hidden in cotton.
- Movement is like drawing silk.
- Action mimics the cat.
- Change begins with a careful mind.

Translated by Professor Zude Ye

Simply put, internal martial arts work to improve the awareness of the subtle energy changes within the body. The aim is toward the conscious direction of these subtle energies. In this way its exponents expect to achieve the best possible standard of health.

Other theories and therapies

Connections between Reiki and the I Ching

About the I Ching

The original texts of the I Ching, commonly translated as the Book of Changes, is credited to Fu His the first Chinese Emperor, in or around 3000 BC.

About 1150 BC King Wen composed a set of judgements to the hexagram and, on his death; his son completed the work by adding interpretations to the individual lines.

Throughout Chinese history great philosophers, alchemists, magicians and mystics have used and translated the I Ching into their own beliefs. The Art of War, by Sun Tsu, has its origins in the Book of Changes as does the Taoist exercise system of T'ai Ji Quan.

Men who had uncommon knowledge, who knew the hidden springs of the future, composed the set of writings known today as the I Ching. This means that they were able to discern the first indications of change, that they could clearly differentiate the real from the false. These men were the sage kings of antiquity, who possessed spiritual power yet lived in the world: they understood the Tao (the Way) of transformation and the nature of heaven and earth.

They believed that character represented the image of God in man, and was therefore the superior self; that personality was the seat of the ego and instinctive drives, and therefore the lower self; that harmony could be achieved when each performed its proper function, according to the nature heaven had assigned to it.

Through the use of the I Ching, Chinese thinkers sought to understand the true nature of, and the connections between, mankind and the cosmos. More specifically they sought to awaken the human potential formerly blocked by conditioning. Rational thinking, instinct and ego, important faculties in their own spheres, were the main agents of these barriers they decided: the I Ching was their main avenue out of the morass.

The body was seen as expressing tension between the energies of two poles, Heaven (Ch'ien) and Earth (K'un): the Yang, Creative or Heavenly power, and Yin, Receptive or Earthly power travelling up and down the body.

The purpose of the I Ching was to point towards a new attitude by dissolving the old one. This is done via the individual lines (of the hexagrams), representing in a general way, difficulties at different levels of experience.

Simply put, the six lines of each hexagram represent the old restrictive point of view, conditioned by the personality, and at the same time, suggest a more detached attitude toward the situation. It is through this attitude of open-minded awareness that the individual changes come about.

Other theories and therapies

When the particular changes are manifest, the view changes: we have entered the new dimension of being. Habitual thinking will draw us back, as we enter into further situations, but this is the nature of change: for character to increase there needs to be a decrease in personality – old patterns of behaviour sacrificed – in favour of a wider and clearer viewpoint.

The above is of course a much-simplified version of the workings of the I Ching. It does not take into account, for example, the image of the hexagram as a whole, or the energy represented by the trigrams and their symbols. Also each change has its own time, and cannot be instigated by self-will.

Expanding this principle helps us to understand the workings of Universal Energy- which is the Divine power of Reiki.

The I Ching tells us that, in knowing the Way (Nature / Essence) of Heaven, we can harmonise with it in the world: that this harmony is achieved when we live in concert with the time.

I hope that you can gain a basic understanding of the mechanism of the book, and a view of the potential for individual fulfilment, from this brief summary. For a more in-depth study of the I Ching you might read, Richard Wilhelm's excellent translation, Thomas Cleary's, *The Taoist I Ching*, or my own text, *Guide to I Ching*.

I Ching and Reiki

Reiki healing can be an important part of the individual's self-development process. By self-development I mean, his or her growth toward inner accomplishment. This implies expansion of character, or higher self, as opposed to personality, which is the lower self.

To have accepted the great responsibility of healing thyself, as well as others through the willingness to be a channel for the Universal Energy, Ki, Chi or Holy Spirit of God is to have already accepted a daunting task.

In Reiki healing the Intelligent Force of Ki follows its own direction: healing by its own will. Thus we sacrifice the personal will: as healers we allow this process to be channelled through us, via the laying on of hands. We are not strictly the healers even, only the agents of the Intelligent Force under whose direction we work.

The great faith of every Reiki exponent then is that there is, 'a body of universal principle', underlying all appearances.

The changes occurring through this faith, plus the work that expresses it, make possible the journey of self-development. This is where the Book of Changes can be of use; it was for this purpose the ancient sage-kings wrote it.

Other theories and therapies

I have chosen some useful examples to demonstrate the connections between the energies of Reiki Healing and the philosophy of the I Ching.

This first hexagram is called Fire, and is number thirty in the sequence of hexagrams. It is composed of six lines as shown, which are:

Yang   —
Yin   — —
Yang   —
Yang   —
Yin   — —
Yang   —

The hexagram is divided into two trigrams, each of which is a symbol for fire. Therefore we have the idea of Fire rising upwards with constancy. In a spiritual context, this applies to the original energy within mankind: it is the essential substance of man's mystical quest.

Fire, twice repeated, means illumination both within and without. Having brightness within is having clear insight: an intuitive knowledge of the Reality of Truth. Brightness without indicates, the correct manner in which character is expressed. This is illumination that travels far: one sees great distances (see clearly what has been and what will be) and is seen from great distances (the light of ones character). One is known for the correctness of one's actions.

The primary requirement of this hexagram is that we know how to develop this inner light. We are advised to be aware of our actions: that we make them reflections of our character, not of our personality. The energy within, to be used unselfishly, must be used for others, yet wisely: the qualification being that assistance has been asked for. (As with Reiki healing) This is being flexible within and firm without.

The parallels with Reiki are clear: the energy applied is Universal Energy, Ki or Chi; the recipient cannot initiate the healing without prior request.

Spiritual healers in all faiths quite often begin as patients themselves. The journey for the healer/teacher sometimes follows a path of extreme hardships, many times resulting in mental and physical illnesses.

St. Paul suggests that the gift of healing comes to few men, but in Mark's gospel we read that Christ declared,

'...anything is possible for the man of Faith'.

If Faith is the only prerequisite, then this suggests that Faith itself is the gift.

Other theories and therapies

The next example from the I Ching is called Inner Truth (Faithfulness at the Centre). Made up of six lines as shown below:

```
Yang ___
Yang ___
Yin  _ _
Yin  _ _
Yang ___
Yang ___
```

The upper trigram symbolises Wind, while the lower symbolises Lake. The inference is: we can observe the effects of invisible energy, in the same way we can observe how the wind disturbs the water's surface.

The broken lines at the centre provide an opening for inner truth. This Faithfulness (Inner Truth), at the centre of ones being, is strong enough to overcome all other influences to the contrary. These temptations might come through ones own desires or the world at large. The purpose of the Book of Changes is, to make it clear whether this is the correct time for spiritual development, or if other forces mislead us.

If the implication is to move forward: in other words, we are united within, in our desire for the journey: then we should take the next step in certainty that Faith will sustain us.

The next step is development, of ourselves as a channel, and of our consistency in doing what is right and in harmony with Heaven.

If we have faith, but are ignorant of the different forces at work, we will always be drawn into bizarre conclusions. Having, 'the wisdom to know the difference', is a prerequisite of good judgement.

A further requirement is that faith and good judgement apply in all cases: no matter what the situation or the obstacle we are to maintain our commitment to truth.

The product of this hexagram is reflected in the honest influence of ones inner truth on others. This is not the manipulative influence based on egotistical motives; nor is it the kind of controlling influence that comes from jealous desire.

The hidden energy of the hexagram of Inner Truth is Faith and Faith is the gift of healing. Without healing, Faith at the centre is the same as a cold heart.

Leaving our short study of the I Ching, we can perhaps look at other forms or styles of Faith Healing.

Other theories and therapies

Spiritual Healing

The Christian Healing Ministry

...Jesus called the twelve together, giving them power over demons and disease. Sending them out he said, 'Take nothing for the journey, neither staff nor bag, bread or money – and only one coat. When you enter a house leave from that same house. When they reject you, shake the dust from your feet when you leave'

Luke 9/1–5

'...greater things than this you will do...' John 14/12

Christ sent out all of his disciples to conduct healing amongst the poor. Later in Luke we read of a further seventy-two that did the same.

The greater part of the work of the early Christian Church centred on this healing ministry. Mostly, the cures resulted from the laying on of hands of the healer, though, as in Mark 5/30, all that was required was that the woman who was ill should touch his coat. In this case it was her faith that healed her.

In the second reading we are told that, for those who had faith in Jesus, the ability to heal would be greater, even than his own.

Two thousand years later it might be expected that, for those with Christian beliefs, such miracles should be a daily occurrence. As this is not so we ought to look for the reason.

The decline in the Christian Healing Ministry came about in the same way as it did in Buddhism: noviciates, as well as the faithful, began to lay greater emphasis on Spiritual Healing than on the Spiritual Life. While this might appear to be no great sin on the surface of things, it appears that the Catholic Church viewed its emphasis so dangerous that it was eventually banned.

This was in the sixteenth century (in Europe), by which time Rome had enough power to outlaw all forms of Spiritual Healing as the work of the devil.

Not a particularly clever law in actual fact, they appear to have forgotten that,

' disease suppressed reappears in a different form'.

It ought to be remembered also that the disciples were cautioned to cast out 'demons' as well as to heal more tangible illnesses. Just because belief systems develop and expand, might not mean that the beliefs of old are nonsense.

What might today's version of a demon look like?

The Vatican rulings on the viability of a miracle are stringent and well known, whereas in the Spiritualist Church the opposite is the case: if someone is healed as a result of 'spiritual intervention' then this is to be expected. Whichever extreme we may or may not endorse, it seems that people do seem to be healed in this way.

As a final word to this brief record of Christian Healing, in the Gospels Christ told his disciples to tell

Other theories and therapies

each of those who were healed,
'..the Kingdom of God is near to you'.

There are many explanations for this directive, but if we add to this the fact that Christ passed on his healing ability to all of his many followers, and they to theirs, then again we have a similarity to Reiki.

Spiritual Healers

National Federation of Spiritual Healers

There are as many sceptical explanations for the results of Spiritual Healing, as there are for Reiki. Primarily these include spellbinding (hypnosis) or simply charlatanism (fakery).

For the sceptic there can be no peace, for his difficulty is in his frame of mind, rather than in the content of his belief/disbelief. The sceptic demands proof, but the proof must satisfy his frame of reference. His frame of reference appears to be a closed structure; either this or that must be true. As the kind of proof for Reiki and Spiritual Healing is outside of his structure of belief (which is disbelief) the sceptic must always revert to disbelief (which is his belief structure).

The basis of most scepticism for the above has more to do with the nature of the healing. As both work to restore balance, to the spirit or essence of the human condition, it is difficult to provide empirical proof, except of course where the restoration of balance results in a cure i.e. manifests physically. The problem of course is that we cannot prove the nature of the cure, which means that the claims of the sceptic cannot be refuted.

Both depend on the Universal Life Force, Ki or Chi to provide the catalyst for rejuvenation. Once this process has been activated, the bodies numerous

Other theories and therapies

healing mechanisms can fulfil their purpose.

In healing systems such as the above, the primary method is the laying on of hands. Here, as we have discussed in previous chapters, the healer acts as the channel for the energy, which then passes to the recipient.

The effects on receivers vary enormously, but in the main are described as a profound sense of ease and comfort, sometimes to the point where the patient falls into a deep sleep.

The secondary method used is known as absence or distance healing. The procedure is simple and has been discussed in detail, in the chapter on Reiki Two: it includes imaging, in which the healer sends out an image of health to the recipient. This image might include the person's name or visual likeness, or simply a voice on the phone, or none of these. The healer works with whatever representatives of the recipient are available: it is the healing message that matters.

One of the old maxims for finding a good martial arts teacher is, 'Don't talk to the teacher, talk to his students'. The same goes for healers: talk to the patients – ask around.

Ayurvedic mind/body healing

To heal, in a modernistic sense, implies that we know the problem; that we are able to affect a cure; and can repeat this system of analysis in every case.

In Ayurveda it is necessary to know the nature of the patient, in order to restore balance. In Ayurveda, joy and happiness mean living in the true nature: it would make sense then to perfect a way, through careful observation, for the individual to return to his natural disposition.

The primary constituent of disease in the Ayurvedic system is consciousness. When we consciously identify with anything in the world, we affect our permanent natures. This happens through a process of obligation: when we make a conscious decision to relate our identities (in an emotional and mental sense) to a finite object, then the conscious view of our true realities is lost to us.

Our human nature causes us to covet what we cannot obtain, attempting either by force of will or fantasy to acquire it. The true nature becomes fragmented, as the need for more and varied satisfactions grows: our energies are depleted because we are no longer centred.

The solution, according to Ayurvedic healing, begins with the knowledge that the satisfaction of worldly desires cannot come first. This knowledge comes, in the first instance, because the old viewpoint

Other theories and therapies

fails us, not because we acquire a better philosophy of life, or even a more promising moral standpoint.

Returning to the true self then equals resisting disease: how is this done? According to Ayurvedic healing techniques, the answer is simple: spiritual exercises.

One such exercise is meditation: sitting quietly while repeating a mantra (internally) or concentrating on a symbol. This momentarily breaks into the normal pattern of subjective thinking, providing a space to experience silence. The silence of meditation is more than lack of noise: most thought patterns are emotionally loaded, quite often negatively: it is the key to other parts of our being.

Emotionally driven trains of thought use up energy – uselessly, and allow very little time for rejuvenation: they prevent healthy sleep; driving us into the use and abuse of medication; creating further negative patterns of thought.

Meditation allows a break in this closed system, and in the space we achieve an awareness of true self: in the silence we begin to sense deep relaxation, rejuvenation and sometimes a feeling of happiness.

There are a variety of meditation exercises, including the use of breath, sound and imagery but they all have the same basic purpose- a return to health: and health, in Ayurvedic mind-body healing, means a return to the true self.

Ayurvedic healing, like Taoist healing, is a full and

practical system and includes diet, its own herbal and detoxification methodologies. As with Reiki, the Chakras are the main energy centres. An Ayurvedic practitioner, who will have studied for a minimum of six years, can deal with most medical problems.

An excellent book on the subject by David Simon, *The Wisdom of Healing*, brings together insights Eastern healing and the scientific knowledge of the West. (see Bibliography)

Reflexology

Based on the theories of Dr. W. Fitzgerald in the 1920s, the main purpose of Reflexology is to restore the balance of energy flow. Fitzgerald discovered channels, or what he called zones of energy, which could be used to treat areas of disease. The ten channels stretched from the feet to the head, separating the body and the organs into zones.

Reflexology, as a science, dates back to the beginnings of acupuncture and acupressure, in 2500 B.C.

Though Fitzgerald made no connection with Chinese Traditional Medicine, much of his zonal theory mirrors the meridian system.

The word reflex, defines the automatic and unconscious response to stimulation. When the practitioner massages, or otherwise manipulates, the feet of the patient an effect is felt, in the reflected area of the body. Reflexologists manipulate the areas of the feet, relating to the various organs, to remove the blockages to the Chi in those areas.

Shiatsu and Acupressure

This system originated in Japan and is very similar to Chinese acupressure. Finger pressure is the primary medium, but palms, knees and even the feet can be used to apply the necessary pressure.

The main purpose of both of these therapies is to promote and restore the flow of the life force.

Because no needles are used, patients can learn and use some of the simpler techniques.

Both therapies are said to be particularly efficient in repairing respiratory problems such as colds, bronchitis and tonsillitis; mouth disorders, especially toothaches. Also for headaches and migraine, digestive problems and pain resulting from bone and muscle complaints.

Other theories and therapies

Homeopathy

This form of therapy originated in Saxony, 200 years ago. A biochemist by the name of Samuel Hahnemann, decided to experiment with some of the popular drugs of his day, when he was not ill.

On of his first experiments was with quinine, used to treat malaria, and he found that he became quite feverish. He theorised that the symptoms that were accepted as those of malaria, were in effect the symptoms of the body's resistance to malaria.

Repeating the experiments with other drugs gave the same results, and Hahnemann realised that like attracts like. By treating an illness producing certain symptoms with a drug, which produced the same symptoms in a healthy person, ought to bring about a cure.

Continuing his research, Hahnemann discovered that the potency of a homeopathic drug did not depend on its strength. In fact, the more the drug was diluted, his research indicated, the more potent it became.

In the nineteenth century his theories appeared to receive all the proof necessary, when the homeopathic remedies for cholera resulted in far more cures than those of the medical profession.

Trials in the 1970's in Glasgow also seem to have proved the validity of homeopathic remedies. If the trials are indeed correct, the necessity for powerful drugs, which have harmful side effects ought to be a thing of the past. The only so called negative reaction from homeopathic drugs appears to be in the nature of purgative effects, such as diarrhoea and vomiting.

Other theories and therapies

Hypnotherapy

Hypnosis can be trace back to earliest times and continues to be a source of interest and wonder. There is little mystery to it, but there is misunderstanding. This is mostly due to the treatment it receives in books and magazines, television films and of course stage shows.

It has stood the test of time and gained acceptance from the Medical Profession. As we come to understand that hypnosis is no more than an expansion of techniques that we use every day, the irrational fears begin to subside. As with other methods mentioned above, we require accurate information to create this understanding and acceptance.

What follows is a brief but accurate synopsis by Carol Harrison. (see gratitude list at front of the book)

What is hypnosis?
Hypnosis is simply a relaxed daydream condition in which a person remains fully aware of their surroundings and in charge of their actions. Many experts believe that we enter hypnosis as much as 80% of our day. It is as natural as breathing. In fact 15 minutes of hypnosis can be the equivalent of an hour of restful sleep.

Will I be asleep or unconscious while in hypnosis?
When you are in hypnosis you are awake, not asleep. Your mind is still active, your thoughts under your own control. You can hear, speak, laugh, scratch and remember everything that has happened.

Is hypnosis dangerous?
There is nothing dangerous about hypnosis. Many people believe they would be under the control of the hypnotist. In reality, it is you who are in control and can choose not to respond to a suggestion. You can bring yourself out of hypnosis anytime.

Can I be made to do embarrassing things as on T.V. or stage shows?
While in hypnosis you wouldn't do anything that you wouldn't normally do. It is important to remember that the subjects of stage and T.V. are all volunteers, thus willing to be uninhibited while on stage.

Can anyone be hypnotised?
Yes, if they want to be. The only people who cannot reach a formal hypnotic state are those who are too young (babies), those suffering from severe brain damage, or those who wont allow it to happen.

Other theories and therapies

What is hypnotherapy?
To put it simply, hypnotherapy is the practise of working with the unconscious mind while a person is in hypnosis. It is a dynamic therapy suitable for resolving many problems, and in many cases can be very effective in just a few sessions.

What happens in hypnotherapy?
During hypnosis you allow yourself to become relaxed by choosing to respond to the suggestions of the hypnotherapist. In this relaxed condition you are in contact with your subconscious mind, the seat of all emotional and behavioural problems. If we understand that the subconscious mind is about 90% and the conscious mind is about 10%, we can easily understand that it is more effective to work with the subconscious mind. It is now widely recognised by doctors and therapists that mind and body are inextricably linked, and that disease or tension in the mind can lead to the same disease and tension in the body. In hypnotherapy we are able to get in touch with the subconscious mind, and so deal with the cause of the problems directly, rather than with the symptoms.

How many sessions would I need?
This of course depends on the problem. However, many issues can be dealt with in 2-3 sessions.

I know hypnosis is used for weight loss and to help stopping smoking, but can it be used for anything else?
Yes. Think of an area of your life where you are less than satisfied with yourself, and hypnosis can help you improve it. It is effective for fear of flying, stress, improving memory, managing anxiety, resolving relationship difficulties, gaining confidence in public speaking and releasing phobias etc. The list is endless.

CHAPTER 8
Case Files

Reiki Master Jill Thurston

My understanding is that the Reiki Master teaches the traditional hand positions. This ensures that Reiki is passed on without the Master's own variations, giving a traditional basis upon which to build.

However, in his book, *Reiki – The Legacy of Usui*, Frank Petter does say,

'It is certain that every Reiki Teacher instructs, in their own Way, and changes the system so that it fits in with his/her Personal understanding of it.'

I teach the original hand positions, but the new Reiki Healer will find that, at times, intuition will take over and the hands will be drawn to the best position for healing the person treated.

The number of attunements for Reiki One varies: some Masters using four attunements, others using less. I believe that Reiki should be kept simple, and have found that only one attunement is all required for Reiki One. This opens the channel from the Crown to the Heart Centre, through the arms to the hands, and then of course from the hands to the recipient. The Reiki energy comes through us not from us.

An attunement is a special event, both for the Reiki Master and the student. The experiences during the attunement vary from person to person. Some people find that their feet tingle, others their hands, but everyone experiences the energy in some way. Everyone finds the experience to be peaceful and relaxing.

Attunements, and the giving and receiving of Reiki, reach us on all levels: physical, mental emotional and spiritual, balancing our energies and enhancing our lives.

Case Files

Ray Bullock

During my Reiki Two attunement, in which Jill Thurston instructed me in the use of the symbols and mantras, it was suggested that I use the opportunity to practise distance healing (as described earlier).

(You will see references throughout this book to sceptics, and the barriers to open-minded judgments that they suffer from. As this was my own standpoint for many years, my involvement in Reiki and related theories has been limited, by fixed ideas and all of the blocks mentioned. I have learned to open up, with discernment, to new ideas and theories outside of my reference. When it was suggested therefore that I attempt distance healing, which has no logical perspective that I could see, I was willing to give up my logical viewpoint and make my judgements on the outcome.)

I followed instructions and dispatched the energy to a friend. When I asked if anything had occurred at that time, they were able to describe, without prompting, the same experience that most feel after a Reiki healing session – falling into a deep and relaxing sleep, followed by a sense of equally deep calmness.

Also to be noted after Reiki Two was the increased energy flow during hands on healing. While my hands had felt warm during a session, they were now much hotter. As well as this, the heat from the energy would linger in the areas to be healed for much longer.

Case Files

Molly Rubin

Experiences of First Degree Reiki

I first became interested in natural healing after reading a book about invisibility ten years ago. In it the healing energy, which could be created by rubbing the palms together, was explained. Eye complaints, such as myopia were said to have improved after placing the charged hands over the eyes at regular intervals. I remember telling my grandmother who suffered with diabetic retinopathy, and we experimented.

I continued to practise with the positive visualisations suggested in the book for years after.

I suffered with rheumatic pain in many areas of my body, mood swings and hormonal problems since the age of thirteen, which became worse with the use of the contraceptive pill.

In 1996, following a bout of glandular fever, I discovered that I had been suffering from a condition known as candidiases: similar in many ways to ME. I followed a strict diet, took supplements and sought treatment with a homeopathic specialist. On my last appointment, three months after my First Degree Attunement, the candida had disappeared. After years of suffering this felt like a miracle.

In June 2000 I had taken a holiday in County Antrim, Northern Ireland at the home of my aunt. She shared my interest in alternative therapies and was a Second Degree Reiki. She asked me to help out at the Carrickfergus First Alternative Health Fair, and I was glad to go along.

At the fair I met one of her friends who was a Reiki master, and as they worked I could feel the energy. Not surprisingly I was delighted to be offered my First Degree Reiki attunement at the end of the holiday. I was instructed regarding the principles and practices relating to Level One, such as its use for the informal treatment of self, family and friends. (Pets and plants also).

The actual experience I shall not forget too quickly. It took place in the attic room where I had been sleeping: a room used regularly for meditation. The Master laid out Crystals around the room, and I was invited to choose some stones, which I could hold during the empowerment; others were place at my feet to ground me. The Reiki Master, my aunty and I held hands and various angels and spirit guides were called upon to help.

I enlisted the aid of a spirit guide, personal to me, lay down and closed my eyes.

The Master used the power of her voice to create an intense energy above my Chakras, altering the resonance for each one. There was a moment's doubt and then I opened up completely.

I felt an increasing heat in each of the Chakras, which I can only liken to a hot flush, or perhaps after eating red-hot chilli peppers.

I was then asked to stand and my aunt was asked to leave the room while the sacred symbols were given. When my aunt returned I was directed to give Reiki to her, and I chose to treat in the manner I had become accustomed, which was with my hands in contact with the other person. The first treatment was intense from my side: my hands were extremely hot. After exchanging treatment, the session was over and we thanked each other and left.

I remember that when I returned to the room there was a real atmosphere of love there. The red carpet and the sun shining through the skylight created a warm pink glow that enhanced the sense of love and peace.

As I lay back down, I perceived a gentle fluttering motion above me. This was not a trick of the imagination, yet neither was the vision clear, but I am certain that what I saw was an angelic being.

(I had a similar experience when I visited a different Reiki Master for treatment, after a car accident. Again I perceived the fluttering of wings and an impression of the colour mauve.

During the discussion after the session, the Master informed me that a certain guide had been called upon, who was represented by this colour and that archangels had also been summoned.)

After the attunement in Ireland there ensued a twenty-one day period of clearing. As Reiki works on all levels: physical mental, emotional and spiritual:

there were areas within my being that underwent extreme changes.

I continued to treat myself with Reiki, practised meditation, and tried to give myself the necessary space and comfort to allow the complete the process. A part of this process was that I experienced an intense level of grief on the last day. My grandmother had died two months previously and I had been holding onto the grief fro all that time.

During a treatment now I have the sensation of a gentle flow of energy: I may be holding the chest position, for instance, and feel the energy sink to my abdomen.

I also feel the heat in my hands, especially toward the end of a treatment, or when giving Reiki to someone else. Fortunately I have trusting friends on whom I can practise.

I find it suits me to use the twelve suggested positions, and then adjust position and time according to instructions from my Higher Power. I always ask for guidance prior to a treatment, and when these messages or images occur I follow their directions.

When areas that I am treating don't feel as porous to Reiki as others, I tend to depend on the guidance of the Director of this healing energy, which for me is God.

My perception of the power of Reiki is, that it is

unconditional Love, which heals both the channel and the recipient.

After the road accident, many people commented on the speedy recovery of the bruises and lacerations to my face. I had begun self-healing an hour after the crash, and continued with three sessions a day. I also made an appointment with a Reiki Master, as I have already mentioned: within a week there was hardly a mark left.

Mostly, I feel I am extremely fortunate to have been given the chance to heal others and myself, and have complete faith that this will continue.

BIBLIOGRAPHY

VIBRATIONAL MEDICINE, New Choices for Healing Ourselves. Richard Gerber, M.D. Bear and Co. Santa Fe 1996

The Hale Clinic GUIDE TO GOOD HEALTH How to Choose the Right Complementary Therapy. Teresa Hale. Kyle Cathie ltd. Great Britain 1996

RECLAIMING THE WISDOM OF THE BODY, A personal guide to Chinese Medicine. Sandra Hill. Constable London. 1997

THE WISDOM OF HEALING, a comprehensive guide to Ayurvedic mind-body medicine. With a forward by Deepak Chopra. Harmony Books New York. 1997

REIKI. Healing and Harmony through the Hands. Tanmoya Honervogt Reiki Master/Teacher. Gaia Books London 1998

HEALING REIKI. Eleanor Mckenzie. Foreword by Reiki Master Don Alexander. Reed Consumer Books, London. 1998

MASSAGE for pain relief. Peijian Shen. Gaia Books

Ltd London. 1996

CHENG HSIN, The Principles of Effortless Power. Peter Ralston. North Atlantic Books, Berkeley, California. 1989

THE POWER OF INTERNAL MARTIAL ARTS, Combat Secrets

Of Ba Gua, Tai Chi and Hsing-I. B.K. Frantzis. North Atlantic Books, Berkeley California. 1998.

Suggested Further Reading

HEALING AND THE MIND. Bill Moyers. Thorsons, London. 1993

AMBIKA'S GUIDE TO HEALING AND WHOLENESS, The Energetic Path to Chakras and Colour. Judy Piarkus, London. 1993

THE BOOK OF COLOUR HEALING. Theo Gimbel. Gaia Books United Kingdom. 1994

ANATOMY OF THE SPIRIT, The Seven Stages of Power and Healing. Carolyne Myss, Ph.D. Bantam Books Great Britain. 1998

HEALING THROUGH COLOUR. Theo Gimbel DCE., Cert. Ed. MIACT., MIHRC., H.DIP.C.TH. C.W.Daniel co. ltd. Great Britain. 1980

MEDICAL ACUPUNCTURE, A Western Scientific Approach. Edited by Jacqueline Filshie and Adrian White. Churchill Livingstone London. 1998